EARLY CHILDHOOD EDUCATION SERIES
Sharon Ryan, Editor

ADVISORY BOARD: Barbara T. Bowman, Harriet K. Cuffaro, Stephanie Feeney,
Doris Pronin Fromberg, Celia Genishi, Stacie G. Goffin, Dominic F. Gullo,
Alice Sterling Honig, Elizabeth Jones, Gwen Morgan

(continued)

Infants and Toddlers at Work

Using Reggio-Inspired Materials to Support Brain Development

ANN LEWIN-BENHAM

Foreword by Mihaly Csikszentmihalyi

Teachers College, Columbia University
New York and London

Published by Teachers College Press, 1234 Amsterdam Avenue, New York, NY 10027

Library of Congress Cataloging-in-Publication Data

Lewin-Benham, Ann.
  Infants and toddlers at work : using Reggio-inspired materials to support brain
    development / Ann Lewin-Benham.
      p. cm. — (Early childhood education series)
    Includes bibliographical references and index.
    ISBN 978-0-8077-5107-7 (pbk. : alk. paper)
    ISBN 978-0-8077-5108-4 (hardcover : alk. paper)
      1. Reggio Emilia approach (Early childhood education).
    2. Infants—Development. 3. Toddlers—Development. I. Title.
    LB1029.R35L48 2010
    372.21—dc22   2010002449

ISBN 978-0-8077-5107-7 (paper)
ISBN 978-0-8077-5108-4 (cloth)

Printed on acid-free paper
Manufactured in the United States of America

17 16 15 14 13 12 11   8 7 6 5 4 3 2

For my sister **Victoria White Cruickshank**,

my grandson **Meyer Shepard Lewin**,

my grandniece **Zen Rose Cruickshank Kretsinger**,

and

my grandnephew **Albert Sinclair Cruickshank**,

who inspired this book.

Contents

Foreword

How to rear children well has been a problem that most societies have had to face, especially after subsistence moved from hunting, gathering, and farming to increasingly abstract knowledge-based occupations. In the twilight of the Roman Empire, for instance, parents—who for centuries had been teaching their children themselves—found it easier to entrust education to literate Greek slaves. It was a cheap solution and it saved time. Historians have argued that, among the many causes advanced to explain why Rome declined, the failure of educating their children was one of the most likely.

This problem is facing us again now. To save time and money, we cut corners on the training of teachers, and force our children to sit in crowded, ill-equipped schools—waiting for robotic teachers to come on-line—those electronic teaching machines that will finally relieve us from having to waste time on our youth. And this at a time when a child who is not able to play with the abstractions necessary to participate in the new knowledge-economy is going to be left woefully behind.

Yet this should not be a problem. After all, the last 100 years have seen enormous advances in our understanding of how children learn, from the neurophysiology of the maturing brain to the ways children attend to and process information.

The bad news is that these advances have rarely been integrated into education. The schools have preferred to go with tradition—even if universal education has a very short one, and one fashioned on the model of the mass-production assembly lines of the Industrial Revolution—instead of learning how to apply the discoveries of neurology and psychology to the teaching of children.

But there is also good news. A few educators have been able to break free from the constraining traditions of passive rote learning. Maria Montessori, Lev Vygotsky, and the founders of the Reggio Emilia schools in Italy—to mention only a few who have influenced the writing of this book—used the true scientific method by observing closely how children behave, thinking hard about what they saw, and then trying out ways to apply their knowledge so that it would make learning more permanent and effective.

Among these pioneers is the writer of the present book. Ann Lewin-Benham has been concerned about how to engage children in joyful learning all of her adult life. As a teacher in Montessori schools, as the founder and director of a major children's museum, as an early adapter of the Reggio Emilia practices in the United

States, she had ample opportunity to observe how children acquire information. And in this book, informed by her vast theoretical and practical knowledge, she has been able to distill the most important issues involved in learning—from the control of attention, to curiosity and motivation—and to present her conclusions in clear, accessible, engaging prose.

This book does not patronize or talk down to the reader: It assumes that teachers and parents are eager to think hard about how the brain works and children learn. The information is scientifically up-to-date and its implications for education are stimulating to laypersons and professionals alike. Reading this book will forever change the way you think about how children learn.

—Mihaly Csikszentmihalyi

Acknowledgments

The inspiration for this book came from my family. My sister Vicky asked the pivotal question: "What should I do with a toddler?" Answers came every time I was with my grandson Sheppy, my grandniece Zen Rose, or my grandnephew Bertie. When I began to think about the book, Bertie had not yet been born, Zen was 4 months old, and Sheppy was 3½ years old. As I write, Sheppy is almost 8½. Twelve cumulative years watching these beloved children informed this book, along with vivid memories of my son Danny's early years.

The infant/toddler centers and preschools of Reggio Emilia, Italy, have been central to my beliefs about what good education is for children of all cultures and socioeconomic groups. I was privileged to observe in their classrooms just prior to the years when Americans began to arrive in large numbers. Their philosophy resonates with everything I believe about human nature, their practices are highly evolved, and their schools are aesthetic, with children's work exceeding what most believe can be created by children 6 and under. I used their publications extensively for insight on how Reggio educators listen to children and for the extraordinary documentation of their projects.

Jennifer Azzariti, the Studio Teacher who worked at the Model Early Learning Center, inspires me. As an artist she brings enormous creativity to projects with her two sons, Louis and William. I marvel whenever I am in their home at what the collaborations between mother and sons have yielded in so many media. She has a selective eye in finding and combining materials that spark children's imagination. This is evident in the schools where she consults. The exquisite detail that pervades the children's work is her signature.

Kate Zieleniewski—Director of the World Bank Children's Center in Washington, DC—graciously opened the school to give me access to teachers, children, classrooms, and loan of the amazing daily journals kept by dedicated teachers. I spent extensive time with Program Specialist Patrick Manning and Yasmin Shaffi, Senior Program Specialist of the Eye Street site. Studio Teachers Elly Solomon and Jessica Gagliardi granted lengthy interviews, showed me extensive work, and provided scores of images. Infant teachers Cecilia Etchegoimberry, Krystal Walker, Lisa Grell, Laura Wright, and Susan Carney, and toddler teachers Zaida Revilla and Dori Weathersbee, welcomed me among their children and answered innumerable questions. Linda Roberts, Administrative Coordinator, provided essential information. The book is rich in detail because of the creative work they have done and their support of this project.

Jennifer Azzariti read many drafts of the book. Holly Blum, an experienced educator, and my niece Alexandra Cruickshank (Zen's mother), in her first years of teaching at the Boulder Journey School, both commented astutely on the manuscript. My husband, Robert Benham, supported me with pithy comments, great fortitude, and chocolate.

Marie Ellen Larcada is a break-the-mold editor; she is the only person with whom I exchange emails who answers as soon as I write. She is untiringly available, helpful, and wise. Her belief in this book is the reason it exists.

The editorial staff at Teachers College Press is top-notch. Karl Nyberg, Senior Production Editor, and Myra Cleary, copyeditor, are endlessly knowledgeable and patient.

I thank the World Bank teachers, Jennifer Azzariti, Alexandra Cruickshank, and Michael Cruickshank—all able photographers—for the images.

Finally, I appreciate the efforts of many brilliant scientists—Mihaly Csikszentmihalyi, Reuven Feuerstein, Howard Gardner, Rochel Gelman, Eric Kandel, David Perkins, Steven Pinker, Robert Pollack, Michael Posner, John Ratey, Oliver Sacks, and Frank Wilson—whose writings guided what I have written about the brain. They and numerous others are forging new paths that hopefully will influence classroom practice.

The last word goes to David Hawkins who, with his wife Frances, did two extended residencies at the Capital Children's Museum during my years as its President. His essays offer timeless insight into the minds of children, the art of great teaching, and the heart of the best educational philosophy.

Introduction

Do you wonder what the random eye movements of a newborn mean? Why 2-month-olds' arms flail in all directions? Why 6-month-olds grasp, bang, and drop? Do you shrink from 2-year-olds' seemingly constant motion? Do toddlers' utterances leave you confused? In these seemingly inexplicable behaviors you are watching the brain make its immense innate capacities operational. Children from 0 to 3 use everything at their disposal—objects, experiences, people—as props for their brain's development. The performance is as awesome as Martha Graham's or Magic Johnson's, perhaps more so. Those maestros were trained and practiced their moves for decades. Infants and toddlers create themselves, with their parents' love but without professional instruction, in 3 years.

In this book I explain what happens when the infant/toddler brain intersects with a wide array of materials. I present teachers who understand that children are competent from the moment of birth and who see strengths that often go unnoticed. I showcase infant and toddler competence to emphasize the importance of opening a world of possibilities that lay the groundwork for their development. I describe the role of materials in helping infants and toddlers fulfill the potential, which is part of every human's heritage, for creative endeavor.

The impetus for the book came from my sister Vicky whose granddaughter, Zen Rose, was 4 months old at the time my grandson Sheppy was 3½ years old. While holding the baby, Vicky watched the preschooler. He was intensely engaged cutting papers into tiny scraps. Some were shiny; others were variously colored or multipatterned. He folded the scraps into even tinier bits, and skillfully tucked them into miniature, transparent, narrow-necked bottles. The effect was beautiful. We added the bottles to the Thanksgiving centerpiece.

"I don't know what I'm going to do when Zen Rose is Sheppy's age!" Vicky exclaimed. "I wouldn't want to resort to putting her in front of TV; I know that's not good. Why don't you write a book about what you're doing with Sheppy?" So, the idea was born.

I was initially a Montessori teacher. Later I founded and for 20 years ran a major children's museum in Washington, DC, where I designed large-exhibit environments on varied themes—pattern and shape, human communication, mechanics, and cultural diversity. We created intriguing spaces that induced children to explore, and we devised activities that encouraged children to use their hands in countless ways. The museum became a destination for families from throughout the world. On the spacious top floor of the museum's rambling buildings I founded and directed the Model Early Learning Center (MELC). It served Head Start-eligible 3- to 6-year-olds. Its stories are the subject of my first two books.

The MELC was based on the philosophy of the world-renowned infant/ toddler centers and preschools of Reggio Emilia, Italy. It was the only school outside their city ever to receive Reggio's accreditation. The MELC became a Mecca for the first wave of Americans inspired by Reggio practices, and one of the first American Reggio-inspired schools to serve Head Start–eligible children. I call this book "Reggio-inspired" because the only real Reggio schools are in Reggio Emilia, Italy. There the schools began right after World War II; there they continue to evolve. I, like many others, draw inspiration from those schools that, as of this writing, number 50. While most of my professional experience has been with urban children and youth, the Reggio practices and the experiences I relate are effective with all children. The infants and toddlers from the World Bank Children's Center (WBCC), who are featured in several chapters in this book, come from diverse cultures throughout the world.

I decided to write about infants and toddlers for several reasons:

- In the years from 0 to 3 the brain shapes itself in ways that are vitally important for later development.
- In these years interactions with people, objects, materials, and environments have enormous implications for subsequent cognitive, emotional, and physical growth.
- By and large, programs that care for infants and toddlers are not stimulating.
- Most child care centers have questions about how best to make use of the new research on early development.
- Homes that are economically disadvantaged may have so little to feed body and brain that children are prone to failure.
- Most parents are confused by the plethora of products claiming that babies will become intelligent if they watch certain videos or use certain toys.

These circumstances impact what we do with children from 0 to 3.

Yet, we *do* know what to do. I have written this book to give those who care for infants and toddlers a clear picture of successful approaches and to explain why they are successful. I have selected from practices we know are best and connected them to research on how the brain develops. My "to do's" are integrated by four themes—recent brain research, teaching techniques, materials' roles, and what it means to learn.

Research. Research in the neurosciences on how the brain works has expanded rapidly since the 1990s as new technologies enabled researchers to watch the brain in action. In Greek times philosophers or doctors stimulated a person, watched the response, and deduced the cause. But only recently have brain images confirmed (or negated) long-held ideas about what causes responses to stimuli. These images have given us entirely new ideas about how the brain functions. The implications for what we do as teachers and caretakers are significant.

The brain controls the body. Everything—from heart beat and breathing to the work that wins a Nobel Prize and the winner's emotions at the ceremony—is controlled by the brain, much of it without a person's awareness. PET scans and fMRI images reveal the extreme complexity of the brain. These new technologies have solved centuries-old questions of whether mind and body are separate: They are not. The brain is as much an organ of the body as the kidneys or digestive tract—although infinitely more complex (Damasio, 1994). New knowledge has erased misconceptions—that we use only 10% of our brain (untrue, we use it all); that we are right-brained or left-brained (untrue, we are whole-brained); that the brain never changes (untrue, throughout our lives the brain rewires itself in response to experience). Scientists actually have watched as brain mechanisms—neurotransmitters, chemicals, and molecular activity—focus attention, control imitation, create memories, respond to stressful or joyful experiences. Brain cells have a special name; they are called *neurons* and are found throughout the nervous system. We now know there are more potential connections among neurons than there are atoms in the universe. We also know there is much we do not yet understand at the deepest levels of brain functioning.

Teaching Techniques. The second theme of the book is various teaching/caretaking techniques that enhance the brain's innate strengths. I explain the importance of the design and organization of an environment and the need to carefully select the materials in it. I show how specific techniques, like modeling, help the brain grasp complex actions. I tell stories of caregivers who know how to listen and observe, who are skilled at determining what activities really interest each child, who are intentional at engaging children in complex activities, and who do so with joy. Intention is possibly the most important aspect of a teacher's behavior; it means knowing what you intend to do and communicating that intention clearly and with authority to children. Intentionality means a teacher will do anything necessary to ensure that she engages children's brains so they are "in flow"—the idea proposed by psychologist Mihaly Csikszentmihalyi that means a state of total concentration resulting in joy and peak performance. I explain the interaction between a child's interest and the brain's attention systems.

Materials. The third theme is how to use many different materials with infants and toddlers. Materials are props for infants and toddlers to develop their brain. But far more! Materials arouse what Dr. Frank Wilson (1998), neurologist and author, calls "the unique human capacity for passionate and creative work" (p. 6). Passion in infants and toddlers? Absolutely! When they stare intently and repeatedly at something, quiver in anticipation, when they smile with their entire face, or concentrate with every fiber of their being, when their breathing and heart-rate quicken, we are seeing the roots of passion. Likewise, when they grapple with the hand movements necessary to do *anything*—maneuver their fist into their mouth, use their eyes to direct their hand toward an object and actually grab it, wield a paintbrush, or nip a chunk off a block of clay around the age of 6 months—we are seeing the roots of creative endeavor: *Use of the hand trains the brain to plan.* To do anything, Wilson says, we need precision in hand and finger grips and a logically sequenced story.

By 14 months toddlers have begun to use many hand/finger grips. Their actions reveal the stories they are telling: See car, as the toddler looks at it; pick up car, as he reaches for, grasps, and lifts it; make car go, as he moves it forward—narrating what he does. If not at 14 months then around 18 months toddlers add increasingly more descriptive words: "Beep, beep!" Or, "Go fast!" Or, "Look out!"

The materials we provide from 0 to 3 determine what finger grips children will use and what stories they will tell. The purpose is not to create "artsy" products but to develop the hand skills that are required for any endeavor, because movement occupies the same real estate in the brain as thinking. Because each material causes children to move the hand in different ways, materials powerfully stimulate thinking (Ratey, 2002). Diverse materials are equally important to awaken interest in different children. From birth each child is unique; each group and each individual has different interests. Having varied materials ensures that there is something for everyone.

Learning. The fourth theme considers what we want infants and toddlers—and older children as well—to learn. Ellen Galinsky, president and co-founder of the Families and Work Institute (2009), located in New York, concerned as we all are about economic and energy crises—and I would add the crisis in global peace—has determined that *the* "crisis in learning" underlies all the others. Galinsky (2010) says seven specific skills engender lifelong learning:

- Focus and self-control
- Perspective-taking
- Communicating
- Making connections
- Critical thinking
- Taking on challenges
- Self-directed, engaged learning

Galinsky and her colleagues have distilled these skills from the work of leading scientists, including Dr. T. Berry Brazelton, Dr. Rochel Gelman, Dr. Alison Gopnick, Dr. Elizabeth Spelke, and more than 70 others. The skills are reflected in activities pictured throughout this book.

A vital source for ideas about learning from 0 to 3 is the educators in the Reggio infant/toddler centers, widely regarded as the world's best. Since 1945 they have generated a philosophy and set of practices that encourage in children from 0 to 3 (and 3 to 6) a great flowering of intelligence. Children in Reggio schools far surpass others of the same age in the range of endeavors they and their teachers undertake and the quality and quantity of their expressive work. The latest findings in neuroscience support the effectiveness of Reggio practices. In this book I use many examples from Reggio schools and explain how their teachers engage children in significant work that is creative, original, complex, competent, and joyful.

CHAPTER OVERVIEW

Chapter 1 shows 0- to 3-year-olds' capacity to become deeply involved as they work to fulfill maturational imperatives, also called basic drives, forces as vital as breathing. Imperatives include moving, coordinating hand and eye, using language, forming relationships with others, and undertaking and accomplishing increasingly complex tasks. To fulfill these and other imperatives, the brain continually sets challenges for itself. Through these tasks neurons develop into networks and networks into highways that must connect in order for the brain to develop. As networks form, random eye movements focus and flailing arms move with increasing purpose. Basic to all learning is attention. In this chapter I describe maturational imperatives and research on the brain's attention systems.

In Chapter 2 I explain *framing*. By framing I mean alerting the brain that something is about to happen and sequencing a task so that its logically related steps are apparent. Being alerted is the first stage of the brain's paying attention; then, a logical approach guides the brain in accomplishing the task. Something seemingly as simple as opening a door actually can be broken into nine steps; miss any one and the door remains closed. A toddler's life is filled with confronting and mastering such complexities. The more clearly tasks are sequenced, the greater infants' or toddlers' likelihood of success. I use examples showing common materials—glue, tempera paint, scissors alone, scissors and paper, and needle, thread, and fabric. If children learn how to "frame," they can approach any task.

In Chapter 3 I discuss infants only up to about 12 months. I describe a 3-week-old infant playing a game using the capacity to imitate, which is a function of movement, one of the brain's most basic systems. I describe a 5½-week-old having a "conversation." A brain function underlying these games is reciprocity, the drive for social engagement that connects an infant to mother, the primary caregiver, and to others. The 5½-week-old has no idea what parts of her body must move in order to vocalize; yet, in 20 minutes, she learns. In this chapter we see teachers who meet maturational imperatives by using common materials to provoke infants' sensory awareness—a range of foods; paper and fabric; objects that bang, clang, and clack; and many found objects.

The core value of the Reggio schools is that a culture of learning is based on multilayered relationships that sustain the individual, a school, and a society. In Chapter 4 I focus on man-made materials and draw a connection between how we use materials and our basic values. Human life depends on materials but today's materialistic cultures are far removed from cultures that gathered and made whatever was needed. Our ancestors did this by developing highly sophisticated and socially driven ways of using the hand. I believe that our divorce from "hand-smarts" is an underlying cause of many problems, individual and cultural. After an eye-opening look at the nuances Reggio educators find in materials, I conclude with the story of a dramatic Reggio infant/toddler experience and descriptions of the creative materials made by infant/toddler teachers at the World Bank Children's Center (WBCC) in Washington, DC. The theme of the chapter is the relation between culture and learning.

In Chapter 5 I show a teacher using tempera paint for the first time with infants of 5 to 7 months. I describe another teacher who fails in her first two attempts to use tempera with 15- to 19-month-olds, but changes her approach and succeeds. I explain Vygotsky's sociocultural theory, particularly the importance of a teacher's acting with intention. The chapter also emphasizes the importance of teachers' listening as the basis for relationships; how the physical design of a school and its furnishings encourage relationships to form; and how these relationships in turn influence children's painting. It concludes with practical information about techniques to use in tempera painting.

Artists' clay, not play dough, is the focus of Chapter 6. I begin with the story of a 6-month-old, hesitant to use clay, and a teacher who uses thoughtful, intentional techniques to help the infant overcome her hesitancy. A second story shows a highly intentional teacher, how he selects a group of four children new to clay, and how he

- structures, frames, and sequences the activities;
- presents new techniques by modeling them himself;
- uses the members of the group to influence and help one another;
- challenges each child in ways that stretch that child's capacity;
- integrates language into the experiences.

The brain functions I explain are the relationship of stimuli to the formation of neuronal networks; the increasing connections among sensory, movement, and communicating neurons; and the three main kinds of cells in the brain.

In Chapter 7 I focus on mark-making, show techniques, and explain why it is as much a maturational imperative as movement and language. I describe a project in a Reggio infant/toddler center where 17 toddlers, ages 2 years, 5 months, to 3 years, drew likenesses of fish. I show how the toddlers' drawings, which bear remarkable likenesses to fish, resulted from a long series of firsthand experiences through which relationships formed among children, fish, materials, and teachers. I describe the typical development of drawing skills and the connections between Reggio teachers' listening and their toddlers' unusual skill.

"Now paper is a marvelous material," says physicist/philosopher/educator David Hawkins. Hawkins describes paper, the focus of Chapter 8, as one of many materials children can use to develop "apperception." Apperception is an understanding of the essence of a material or a phenomenon—how it behaves, responds, and changes. Apperception is gained through repeated use, not to fulfill a goal, but rather to "mess about," something Hawkins (1965) says is essential in order for children to grasp any big idea. I describe experiences at the WBCC using a great variety of papers with infants over the course of several months. Then I describe big projects with paper in Reggio schools with infants 6 to 10 months old and with toddlers 18 to 24 months old. All show paper as a stimulus for complex thought processes, for apperception, and for "mentalese," which psychologist Steven Pinker calls the brain's form of internal communication, nothing like the language in which we express ourselves daily.

One-year-old Zen was fascinated when three ladybugs landed on her. Three-year-olds at the MELC crawled into the mirrored kaleidoscope, found it filled with ginkgo leaves, and saw themselves wrapped in an intense sea of yellowness. Two-and-a-half-year-old Dana saw chicks hatch. She recounted the experience to anyone she could corner! Natural materials, the topic of Chapter 9, include bark, twigs, leaves, seeds, soil, pebbles, pods, water, grass, flowers, and animals. They can powerfully grab young children's imagination. Because color is primary in natural materials, I explain the role of color in vision. The theme is the importance of instilling the wonder of nature during the years 0 to 3.

Light and shadow, the focus of Chapter 10, represent the paradox of being and nonbeing, of entities we can see but not grasp. Because experiences with light and shadow are entirely visual, I explain what happens in the brain as it translates photons—particles of light that hit the retina virtually instantaneously into meaningful information. I describe how to make light and shadow a presence in infant/toddler classrooms and the necessary equipment. I recount six months of infant/toddler experiences with a light table, an overhead projector, and a host of teacher-made materials at the WBCC, and conclude with a description of toddlers' experience using shadows in a Reggio infant/toddler center.

The three big ideas in this book are:

1. Competence. Children from 0 to 3 are extremely competent. As scenarios in this book imply, we wait too long before engaging infants and toddlers in complex experiences. The norm is to bore them with not enough stimulation or to stifle them with the wrong stimulation. I trust that this book provides a third alternative—providing surprising, beauty-full, complex, and joyful experiences through which children from 0 to 3 can set a pattern for lifelong learning.

2. Materials. The second big idea is that certain kinds of materials are essential resources for 0- to 3-year-olds to build the neuronal networks that will form the basis for everything they subsequently do. Materials stimulate the senses, which respond by developing networks in the brain that in time enable us to use high-level brain functions and to build relationships among complex ideas. Materials educate the hand, which drives language, movement, attention, planning, and scores of other essential brain functions. The combination of hand and materials is essential to virtually any endeavor.

3. Relationships. The third big idea is that children form relationships among one another and adults, with materials, with environments, and with ideas *if* teachers listen and observe, use children's own interest as the key to what to offer each individual, and use children's engagement as the basis to develop self-regulation and joy. In the first years of life especially, and at least through age 8 or 10, the most important thing children can learn is how to focus their attention on the accomplishment of big tasks that they themselves take part in defining. I trust that this book makes clear how important it is to develop the attention systems in children's brains so they learn how to learn and thereby harness their brain for whatever creative and ennobling endeavors they conceive.

When their competence is nurtured and their brain is challenged, children will make focus a habit. Self-regulation then "become[s] a way of working that is no longer childish, though it remains always childlike, [but is] the kind of self-disciplined probing and exploring that is the essence of creativity" (Hawkins, 1965, p. 8).

1

Why Use Materials?

> It is obvious that the development of mind comes about through movement.
> —Maria Montessori (1967)

Alex, age 16 months, reached haphazardly for toy after toy, neither looking at nor playing with one before he reached for the next. Roland, age 10 months, squirmed when held to look at a book. Jenny, age 2½, zoned out, off in her own world, no matter what conversation an adult or a friend broached. None of these children was focusing. Yet, beginning in infancy children have the ability to become deeply engaged. Deeply engaged children are attending; that is, they are directing their brain to focus on a specific task. Attention cuts across all domains and is an integral part of all other brain systems—movement, language, sensory, cognitive. We can't think, learn, or do anything without focusing our attention. The premise of this book is that materials play a pivotal role in motivating children and stretching their capacities to focus and sustain attention.

Research shows that infants attend, but once something loses its novelty they become bored. Psychologist Mihaly Csikszentmihalyi (Chik-sent-muh-hī) uses the word *flow* for total concentration on anything that stretches our capacity; flow is characterized by a "fine balance of challenges and skills" (1993, p. xiii). Flow is the basis for happiness, creativity, peak performance, development of talent, productivity, self-esteem, and stress reduction (pp. 192–195). In this book we see numerous scenarios with infants and toddlers in flow as they use varied materials.

In Chapter 1 I discuss the brain's attention system and the relationship between materials and development. I describe maturational imperatives that are present in infancy. Maturational imperatives are ways the brain drives the body with little outside stimulation—like the boot programs that bring computers up when we turn them on. Harvard psychologist Elizabeth Spelke calls this "core knowledge" (Spelke & Kinzler, 2007). Infants are born ready to turn on; however, how facile the brain ultimately becomes, depends greatly on the relationships that form among infant, environment, materials, and adults who, in the early years, create the environment and choose the materials. Here I show humans as learners, describe the relationships between specific maturational imperatives and materials, and explain the role of materials from 0 to 3. I conclude the chapter with a description of the role of structure in collecting, organizing, and containing materials.

INFANTS AND TODDLERS IN FLOW

Any time we think about anything, we first must alert our attention. The attention system is a hot topic in brain research, and information about it is accumulating at a rapid pace. Here I present a bit of that research and explain its relation to adult interactions with infants and toddlers.

Research on Attention

Neuroscientist Michael Posner (2004), considered the leading authority on attention, says: "Attention is being studied at the cognitive, neuro-system, cellular, synaptic, and genetic levels. . . . Like other organ systems, attention has its own anatomy, transmitters, and development" (p. 3). Researchers around the world are doing the microresearch that, as it accumulates, forms the big picture of how the many complex subsystems involved in attention work and interact.

> Different research groups, and their models, differ somewhat in the way they subdivide and term components of attention. However, they all recognize the importance of: 1) a basic level of arousal and alerting; and 2) a selective focus on specific stimuli and signals, to further process these signals, either transiently or in a sustained manner. (Neville et al., 2008, p. 107)

Selective Focus. This vitally important part of the attention system creates and uses the strength of selected signals. These signals are either increased or suppressed by chemical transmitters that are called impulses (a different meaning of the word than reaching for a piece of chocolate). ADHD is a symptom that something is amiss in the attention system, that children may not be selecting or suppressing stimuli adequately.

> Studies exploring how the process of attention develops have documented that it matures over a prolonged period of time. This is the case even for aspects of attention that may be present in some form in infancy. Therefore, while alertness is clearly present in infancy, the ability to remain alert for effortful processing has a protracted developmental time course, that extends into young adulthood. (Neville et al., 2008, p. 108)

As an executive function of the brain, attention makes it possible for children, beginning in infancy, to orient themselves to an experience and maintain focus on it. These behaviors underlie children's abilities to become self-disciplined, to focus on a task, to see it through to completion, and to maintain concentration.

> It is quite amazing that infants of 3–4 months can be taught to orient to places in the environment in advance of presenting a stimulus at that location. (Posner, 2004, p. 6)

This shows that

executive attention is present in infancy, and can be measured . . . by assessing [infants'] anticipatory looks. (Posner, Rothbart, Sheese, & Kieras, 2008, p. 7)

Components of the Attention System. Teachers are not "measurers"; they are gatekeepers between research and classroom. If teachers know the components of the attention system, they will be better prepared to incorporate them into activities. The components of attention are complex assemblies of neurons that enable us to

- attend to incoming stimuli,
- filter out distractions,
- select one stimulus over another,
- juggle multiple perceptions to determine which is the most important,
- sustain attention (or stay focused),
- plan how to achieve a goal,
- extract meaning and attach emotion,
- store what we need in memory, and
- manage all these activities in real time.

Researchers have identified and watched three separate brain networks that alert, focus, and manage attention (Alvaro, 2008). The management is called self-regulation; it means an individual's watching and controlling how he himself is thinking or behaving. "Research suggests that genetic markers may exist that help explain differences seen in children's abilities to selectively focus attention for effortful control of cognition and emotion" (Posner et al., 2008, p. 7).

The teacher's role is to understand that materials alert the brain and cue selective focus. Therefore, teachers must be sure that the materials they offer, which are stimuli to the brain, have characteristics that in fact *can* alert and rouse children's interest and evoke sustained attention.

Attention and Materials

Open-ended materials are especially important because they allow many approaches; therefore, they reach children with diverse interests. They also stimulate long engagement. Long engagement is evidence of sustained attention. Some may dismiss the materials and experiences I describe as "art" and thus irrelevant to learning. Nothing is less true. After 3 years of research on how the arts influence other cognitive processes, the Dana Foundation found significant connections through the underlying mechanism of attention. Their research identified "the neural network (system of connections among brain areas) from among the several involved in attention that is most likely to be influenced by arts training" (Posner et al., 2008, p. 1). Any activity that trains attention builds the brain's capacity to learn. And that—enlarging the capacity to learn—is the reason for using materials.

I refer throughout this book to "materials," not "arts," because materials are the basis for science, mathematics, or any endeavor that requires the brain to make connections, see cause and effect, set and reach goals—in other words, to think. I define materials broadly to include symbol systems and intangible modes of thinking; so, for example, sound, gesture, and the symbols that represent them (musical notes, iconic signs in public places, letters) are "materials"—they are part of the wherewithal that the brain uses to think. All the materials I describe, when used by intentional teachers, have the capacity to build sustained attention. They also embody complexity, which ultimately builds systems in the brain that are both differentiated in structure or function and integrated so that they "communicate and enhance one another's goals" (Csikszentmihalyi, 1993, p. 156).

HUMANS: UNIQUE LEARNERS

A debate for millennia has been whether humans develop because of nature or nurture. Current thinking is that both play vital roles but development is far more complicated than formerly recognized because the brain, "a complex device, can tune itself to unpredictable aspects of the world and take in the kinds of data it needs to function" (Pinker, 1997, p. 33). The brain is composed of many systems, each with its own many subsystems, all the way down to the genes, and all connected by chemicals with their own multiple levels of systems. Add to this the complexity of all the outside influences that accumulate from the moment an embryo is conceived, and you get some sense of the brain's complexity (Damasio, 1994). Trauma to a system before, during, or after birth or genetic causes can derail the drive or hamper the capacity to learn. While there are broad outlines for how humans develop, the specific path for any infant is highly individual because the mix of environment, human interactions, and the infant's own temperament is incalculably intricate.

Theories of Development

Research on children from 0 to 3 concurs: "What happens during the first months and years of life matters a lot . . . because it sets either a sturdy or fragile stage for what follows" (Shonkoff & Phillips, 2000, p. 5).

Materials' Role. For centuries, children were considered simply small, immature adults. The special nature of young children's brain was not understood. Then, Jean Piaget proposed a new theory: Children learn as a result of using the *things*—that is, the materials—in their environment. By mid-20th century, his theory began to influence schools, toy manufacturers, and parents as the idea of learning-through-doing captured public attention. Classroom materials became common, especially in arithmetic. Materials were developed to teach specific concepts like color, shape, number, and many other abstract ideas. Children's museums opened everywhere based on the idea of hands-on learning-through-doing. Piaget's insight remains the basis for many ideas about how we learn. But . . .

Humans' Role. No sooner had Piaget's ideas become influential, than a newer theory about how we learn came to light. Russian psychologist Lev Vygotsky theorized in the 1920s that children's interactions with other humans are the critical component in learning. Vygotsky was born in 1896 (the same year as Piaget), but died of tuberculosis at age 38 and his ideas did not spread until after the Cold War. Some of his ideas are talked about more than they are used. Psychologists who study how infants and children learn have retained Piaget's idea of the importance of using materials as learning aides. But followers of Vygotsky, many of whom are leading psychologists, believe that materials have most influence on learning *when they are used together with another human*. More than just together with, children learn best when an adult interacts in the process of using materials and when learning takes place as a social, or collaborative, process. Current research in neuroscience confirms many of Vygotsky's theories.

Psychologist Reuven Feuerstein has developed a robust theory, called the Mediated Learning Experience, to explain what happens in adult/child interactions. Briefly, mediation is any intervention by an adult with intention (I *require* you to focus your attention), meaning (the significance of this stimulus is . . .), and transcendence (what we are doing relates to something in the past or future) (Feuerstein, Feuerstein, Falik, & Rand, 2006). Bookmark this page because I identify examples of intention, meaning, and transcendence throughout the book. Feuerstein uses materials, which he calls stimuli, to alert attention, sustain focus, and convey meaning.

The Role of Evolution

Genetically, infants are *wired* to learn and their parents are *wired* to help them. The innate tendency of parents to teach is essential for human survival. Babies in other species, almost from birth, can do what they need to survive: eat, climb, run. The size of the human head in relation to the body is larger than in any other animal because our brain is larger. However, human babies have by far the longest development outside the womb to learn how to survive. This resulted millennia ago from a compromise as humans evolved.

For the forerunners to our species to stand upright, the size of the pelvis had to change. As the physical structure changed, the pelvis grew too small for a fully grown human head to pass through the birth canal: Were the fetus to remain in the womb until its brain fully developed, gestation would last for years and the infant could not get out! "Fetal brain growth [continues] for a year after birth. If our bodies grew proportionally during that period, we would be ten feet tall and weigh half a ton" (Pinker, 1997, p. 183). Because we are born before brain development is complete, materials, experiences, and other humans play major roles in determining *how* the brain develops.

SITTING, WALKING, CARRYING

The senses are set to go at birth and systems in the brain are equipped to develop unique human capacities in language, music, movement, fashioning objects, and other complex acts; these depend on brain/eye connections and movement of many parts of the body, especially the hand. All of these systems become evident in maturational imperatives, the innate drive to learn that defines humans. I divide infant/toddler development into three periods—before 6 months, before 18 months, and before 3 years—and discuss the role of materials in each.

Infants Before They Sit

Materials fascinate infants almost from birth. Some tickle or scratch. Others are wet, dry, rough, or smooth. Textures are pleasing—soft, furry, warm, velvety, silken. Sights are mesmerizing—the high contrast where black and white touch, the angles where ceilings and walls meet, the intricate network of bare tree branches, the colors and aromas of a garden in bloom, humans' faces, animals' eyes, the shape of an elephant, the size of an ant. Sounds are intriguing from infancy. Is it deep and booming or high and tinkling? Is it musical? Are sounds rhythmic? Do they make rhymes? Do they tick, dong, bang, or bark? Smells are familiar—mommy's body, daddy's shaving lotion, milk, the dog's odor, an orange's pungency, a baking cake's spices. Tastes are strange—strong, mild, pleasant, sweet. Movements are soothing—rocking, patting, hugging, nuzzling; or terrifying—falling! Maturational imperatives, such as movement and sensing, begin to play active roles in learning even before birth. Perceptual modes active in the womb include: tactile, visual, auditory, olfactory (smell), gustatory (taste), haptic (touch/movement), and proprioceptive (knowing where parts of your body are spatially).

The teacher's role in the first 6 months, before infants sit alone, is to use materials in greatly varied experiences that appeal to all the senses (see Chapter 3) and to provide a wealth of opportunities for infants to explore through unrestricted movement. The importance of moving freely—in clothes and space that are not confining—cannot be overemphasized: Movement is infants' response to stimuli that are received through the senses. Restricting movement restricts the ability to construe meaning from experience. Meaning-full stimulation, freedom of movement, and an engaged adult set the stage for learning.

Staring. A huge tree stood outside a window directly in the line of sight from Sheppy's cradle. He was born in February in a cold climate so the branches were bare. For months he stared fixedly and for long periods at the intersecting lines that, on windy days, danced for his pleasure. Sheppy also stared fixedly, his gaze intense, in early mornings when I held him in my bed before we both dozed off for a bit more sleep. I maneuvered my face next to his to track what he found so mesmerizing. Sometimes it was the bold lines of the plaid on the duvet cover, other times the corner where two walls and ceiling met.

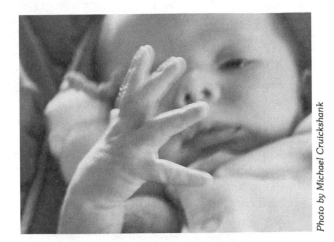

This 3-week-old infant staring at his hand with sustained and focused attention represents every infant's drive to figure out the world by using innate systems in the brain and experiences in the environment.

Photo by Michael Cruickshank

Infants' fixed staring builds the visual system. When you watch where a baby stares, you can modify the environment. Jennifer Azzariti, the first Reggio-inspired studio teacher in the United States, propped oversize books, magazines, maps, and other large high-quality graphics in her infant son's line of vision. Research by Spelke (1990) and others shows that when objects are different, new, or surprising, infants stare longer. Light, mirrors, and objects that glisten or move alert the visual system and cause infants to sustain their attention.

Pointing. Pointing is a uniquely human way for one person to share something with another. If you want an infant to notice something, call his attention by pointing at it. Extend your arm, point your index finger, and follow your finger tip with your eyes, staring hard. Then, engage the infant's eyes. Once you have engaged his eyes, shift his attention along your arm toward your finger. This powerful stimulus to focus on the act of pointing follows the maturational imperative to pay attention to movement, and by 9 to 12 months leads to sharing ideas with another person (Feuerstein et al., 2006; Spelke & Kinzler, 2007).

Imitation. Infants imitate naturally and will readily copy movements within their capacity. At age 40 Alice adopted her first child, a 6-month-old girl. She introduced an appealing stuffed toy, intended as a sleep object, but her baby was not interested. So, Alice lovingly cuddled the toy, cooed to it, stroked it, then handed it to the baby, who immediately took and cuddled it. It is easy to *teach* infants specific actions through imitation.

Staring, pointing, and imitation are among the ways infants learn. Spelke's theory of core knowledge says that mental "modules," in place at birth, build "mental representations of objects, persons, spatial relationships, and numerosity. . . . [They] enable infants to organize their perceptions [and] underlie all the more complex skills and knowledge we obtain and master as we grow up" (in Dobbs, 2006).

Infants Before They Carry

This is the period from 5 to 7 months—when infants' hands grasp well and they begin to sit—and 14 to 18 months—when they walk and carry simultaneously. Huge developments take place. By intentionally using well-selected materials, adults tap maturational imperatives and stimulate the growth of neuronal networks.

Hand. In infancy the hand's capacity expands rapidly. Neurologist Frank Wilson (1998) explains growing evidence from neurology and paleo-physiology: Changes that ultimately produced the human hand spurred a "redesign, or reallocation, of the brain's circuitry" (p. 59). To use your hand, you must anticipate, carry through, and conclude an action. The new brain thus would require "new ways of registering and representing the behavior of objects moving and changing under the control of the hand. It is *precisely* such a representational system—a syntax of cause and effect—that one finds at the deepest levels of the organization of human language" (p. 60, emphasis in original). Wilson concludes that as infants begin to explore with their hands, they activate the parts of the brain that develop language.

As neuronal networks grow, infants set new goals for themselves. For example, this 19-week-old, lying on the grass with daddy, spies his cat and intends to grab it. To do so he must coordinate eye/head, head/body, arm/shoulder, eye/arm/hand, and eye/hand in a particular sequence and must move in a particular trajectory at a specific speed in order to grab the stimulus—the cat's waving tail.

Stabilizing the head on the neck and the neck on the torso is essential for the eyes to focus and the hand to grasp an object. By 6 to 7 months, infants accomplish these feats.

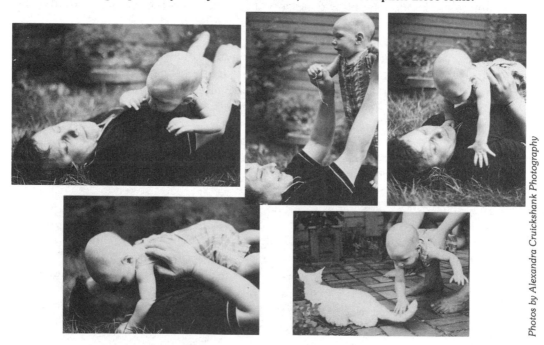

Photos by Alexandra Cruickshank Photography

Photo by Ann Lewin-Benham

Once they can sit and grasp simultaneously, new horizons open for infants.

The brain and body are designed to do these things, but in infancy making everything work together, in sequence, with directionality, and on time, is a high-level challenge. Making such movements effortlessly takes practice. By 28 weeks most infants have the strength and have sufficiently stabilized eye/head/arm/body to sit and reach for objects. When infants master sitting, they command a new visual field, inaccessible from back or tummy. With so much to see and new eye/head/hand abilities, new natural drives flower, like propelling the body forward.

Movement. Movement is a vital life force. Every infant creates movement anew in the interactions between adults, environment, "stuff," and its own brain. When you watch infants' or toddlers' minute-by-minute hand, head, eye, finger, arm, shoulder, and other movements, you are seeing an intentional, focused, "self-disciplined probing and exploring that is the essence of creativity" (Hawkins, 1965, p. 8). Wilson (1998) says that the connections between movement and brain are so synergistic and thoroughly integrated

> that no single science or discipline can independently explain human skill or behavior. . . . The hand [for example] is so widely represented in the brain, the hand's neurological and biomechanical elements are so prone to spontaneous interaction and reorganization, and the motivations and efforts which give rise to individual use of the hand are so deeply and widely rooted, that we must admit we are trying to explain a basic imperative of human life. (p. 10)

Carrying objects in both hands and walking among balls challenge this 14-month-old's ability to balance.

Photos by Ann Lewin-Benham

At 14 months Sheppy's balance was good enough to hold an object in each hand while walking on an even floor. But it required total concentration and outstretched arms to walk on a floor covered with balls in an exhibit at the Carnegie Science Center (Pittsburgh). And, it will be several months before he can carry large objects. On this same visit to the Science Center (at 14 months) a test tube rack with six test tubes caught Sheppy's attention. One by one, over and over he grasped a tube, oriented it, fit it over the upright support, and slid it down. "The child learns with real objects, through trial and error, to make constructions that are concrete events unified through a *sequence* of actions" (Wilson, 1998, p. 195, emphasis added). Wilson equates sequencing objects with telling stories, and, in fact, PET and fMRI images show that the same areas of the brain are active in the sequencing functions of both movement and language.

Language. Language centers in the brain are active long before the physical apparatus that enables children to speak is operational. The first year of life is a "submerged and silent laboratory of attempts, trials, [and] experiments in communication . . . [and] confirms the strong desire to communicate . . . [as] the basic trait of children" (Malaguzzi, 1991, p. 14). Infants love to hear language and can be read books from birth. Language can accompany experiences with any new material: "Can you tear it?" "It's sticky!" "Is it wet or dry?" "This dissolves in water." "Does it tickle?" When adults demonstrate actions, show reactions, and simultaneously describe them, infants will associate word and action and around age 1 begin to form words more readily. In seminal research Janellen Huttenlocher and colleagues (1991) showed that the more talk caretakers directed to infants, the larger their vocabulary was during school years.

The sequence of language development has been widely documented in work begun by Roger Brown who, with his Harvard students, laid the groundwork to un-

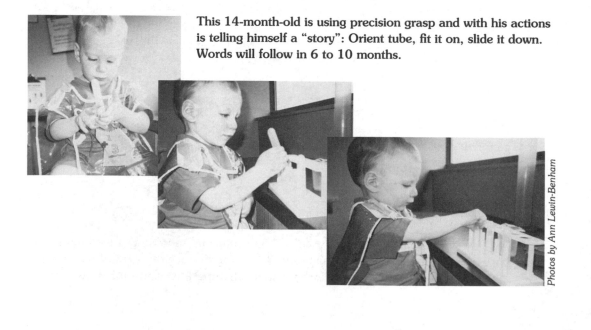

This 14-month-old is using precision grasp and with his actions is telling himself a "story": Orient tube, fit it on, slide it down. Words will follow in 6 to 10 months.

Photos by Ann Lewin-Benham

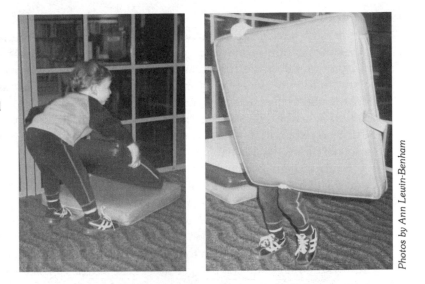

Walking and carrying larger and larger objects is a challenge toddlers set for themselves around the age of 20 months.

Photos by Ann Lewin-Benham

derstand language acquisition. They analyzed countless hours of recordings of vocalization, babbling, and the gradual emergence of words. It is beyond the scope of this book, but is a fascinating story, well worth rereading. Pinker (1994) tells it well.

Toddlers' Walking and Carrying

Between 12 and 20 months toddlers gain increasing control over their balance. Sometime during this period their movement is sufficiently stable for them to walk without needing outstretched arms to maintain balance. This is when toddlers spy the just-ironed load of clothes and gleefully carry it—where it arrives in not-so-ironed condition. It is the age when toddlers carry a blanket or soft toy everywhere or hoist cushions larger than they are. These more challenging maturational imperatives drive toddlers to invent more complex games.

Danny, at 17 months, walked without needing his arms for balance. In the living room was a large nut bowl, and beside each chair was a table with an ashtray. Danny invented a game: distribute the nuts into the ashtrays. It required mastering the skill to carry-while-walking, to maintain balance while holding an object (the bowl) with one arm and doing something different—take-out-nut, put-in-dish—with the other, and to sight a target and drop something into it. He constrained the game by putting only one nut in each dish so that he made numerous trips around the room to empty the bowl. His game provided many challenges to a 17-month-old brain.

Materials as Stimulus

Imperatives to handle, move, and communicate are fostered by interaction with other humans and with materials. The more diverse the stimuli we give infants, the more opportunities they have to fulfill imperatives. Stimuli, however, do not mean a welter of plastic chaos with stuff strewn everywhere. Rather, providing stimuli is the gradual introduction, one at a time, of thoughtfully selected materials. As the hand improves at grasping objects and finding targets, the 3-month-old finds her mouth, which becomes a primary test organ for any material. In Reggio infant/toddler centers infants are given paint and paintbrush as soon as they can sit, hold their balance, and simultaneously hold an object. At this age they begin to explore artists' clay. Not too long after, by 10 months, they are ready for more advanced exploration—physical challenges of steps and ramps, eye/hand challenges of gluing, mark-making, and exploring light.

Many challenges appeal only during the time when they are maturational imperatives. Earlier, infants/toddlers will not respond or will be frustrated. Later they will be bored. When the challenge is just right, children repeat. Repetition, another maturational imperative, enables infants/toddlers to master challenges gradually. Mastery occurs when a brain function, or cluster of functions, has been repeated enough for the brain to habituate the processes. Using materials that engage brain systems *during the time when these systems are developing* challenges the brain, requires it to focus, and makes it possible for brain systems to become integrated and function seamlessly.

From 0 to 3 infants-turning-toddlers-turning-children gain enormous experience from using a variety of materials. As a result they learn more about how their world functions and become more aware, curious, and competent. The purpose is not to make some *thing*, but for different materials to increasingly challenge and integrate the brain's attention system and the eye/hand/movement nexus. As adults offer materials and use them with children, adult/child relationships develop that are playful, exploratory, loving, surprising, and language-full.

STRUCTURING THE USE OF MATERIALS

This book intends to give infants and toddlers a voice, to show how beginning explorations can have structure, use quality materials, and be aesthetic so that they foster an appreciation of beauty. The materials I suggest are not available in baby departments or toy stores. Nor are they found in most child care environments. Neither are explorations I describe part of instruction manuals or teacher guides. Why? While educators are aware that there is new research on the importance of the first years, there is little information about exactly what to do to take advantage of all those firing synapses. Commercial products with titles like "Smart Baby" and "scientific" claims have filled the void. Many are "watch-me/hear-me" products comprising visual stimulation and/or auditory input. They neither provide a role for the integration of brain/eye/body/hand nor build reciprocal relationships between infant/toddler and adult. In contrast, what I describe in this book fosters the brain/eye/hand/movement nexus and builds adult/infant relationships.

There is no exact age for each experience. Something I describe for an older child may be fine for a younger one, or vice versa. Whatever age, if the child has never handled a particular material, the same introductory experience can be used.

For young children there is no distinction between art and science, past and future, process and product. At this age, process *is* the product. *Doing*, for the pure joy of doing, not to make a particular *thing*, is the work and play of infants/toddlers.

Materials provide immediate connections between brain and environment. If a child plays with materials in the first 3 years, her mind will be full of things to do with them. Eighteen-month-old William picked up a bamboo branch and marched it down the street. His teacher asked what he was doing. "Playing the bassoon," he answered. Sheppy, just turned 4, asked me on the phone, "Do you have any wood at your house? Because when I come to Memphis, I want to make a bed for Mimi [his nighttime piglet]. And I need something squishy and some . . . [pause while he searched for the word] fabric." Here I discuss concerns about mess and safety; finding, organizing, and storing materials; and places to work. Appendix A lists commonly available materials alphabetically; Appendix B lists materials carried by purveyors of art supplies; Appendix C lists tools.

Confronting Concerns

What about the mess that can result from using materials? A young teacher commented: "It frustrates me because it gets over the top messy." If you feel an experience is too much, stop. Consider doing a messy activity outside. Painting, one of the messiest activities, raises the issue of discipline. At some ages or with some children, they simply might be slopping, not painting. I do not let children pour out the paint randomly or flick it. Nor do I use paint with extremely oral children who put everything in their mouth. I set behavioral boundaries and make sure to adequately prepare the space. There is a balance—not so strict that it takes away the fun, but a sensitive eye to the line where purposeful activity disintegrates.

What about danger? Many teachers find scissors frightening. Caution: *None of the activities, especially scissors, is meant to be unsupervised.* The point of every activity is to build relationships, not to fill time. If an activity feels dangerous or if you do not have time to give total attention throughout, skip the activity. This book is meant to provide pleasure, not pressure. The experiences included here worked for the children and teachers in different classrooms I ran or observed. They may not work for yours. If in doubt, use your judgment. Most important is for you and your children to share time together with wonder, laughter, and joy.

Finding Good Materials

Jennifer Azzariti doesn't buy much. She scrounges, not to be frugal, but because found objects are more interesting than purchased ones. They have a history. Yard sales and attics are full of stories. Repurposing creates new stories. Any material is great if *you* think it is fabulous or see potential; multiples of anything are better. One teacher noticed that her straw pocketbook was worn; she carefully deconstructed it and salvaged a trove of long, colorful raffia. If you fish, bake, woodwork, sew, or garden, you will understand the process of collecting materials. Gathering materials for your own pursuits is similar to gathering classroom materials. Combing your house probably will yield most of the items in Appendix A—paper, metal, fiber, wood, plastic, cardboard, art and sewing supplies, hardware, packaging materials, and one-of-a-kinds like discarded pieces of jewelry, unusual buttons, or wood turnings. They work for children of many ages.

Exciting materials not necessarily found in homes include silk flowers, cellulose (theater gel material), and industrial leftovers (from manufacturing areas). Block areas in Reggio schools contain cones about 10 inches high made from heavy cardboard; they are empty thread spools from the area's clothing industry. The first photo set in Chapter 4 shows scrap wood turnings used for blocks. Some children's museums collect cast-off manufacturing items and let you fill bags for a few dollars. If you collect materials, you probably examine packaging before throwing it away. Tell me what materials you enjoy that are not included in the Appendices; I'll publish them with your name and comments on my website, AnnLewin-Benham.com.

Most wrappings can be recycled. You can paint, glue, or collage on gift wrap. Avoid wrappings that are printed with commercial "art." Instead use foils, subtle abstract patterns, or papers of interesting color, weight, or texture. If you include holiday leftovers among your materials, choose carefully and make small snips of anything with suggestive colors or strong images so that they do not overwhelm other materials and colors. Anything you do—whether necessities like eating and washing, or hobbies—yields a rich trove of materials.

Organizing Materials

If the number of materials I suggest seems overwhelming, recall TV ads for closet organizers—jumbled clutters whisking quickly into order! The key is organization. Without it, materials *are* overwhelming. I suggest a couple of approaches but there are many. Whatever works for you and your space is best.

As Is. Everything stays where it is as part of your organized classroom. You gather it when needed for activities and return leftovers to their place. Teachers who use this approach:

- Leave room to add new items.
- Find storage space for currently discarded items.
- Designate a "tote-it," some easily portable container-with-handle to take items to and from the work space. A comfortable size holds 8½ x 11" paper without bending or falling out and has a high handle so items come in and out easily. If you always use the same carrier, infants soon recognize that something pleasurable is about to begin.

The brain requires novelty; the tote-it, bringing a special sensation or experience whenever it appears, provides that novelty. Some infants quiver in anticipation on seeing it.

Particular Place. Designate a particular place or places, assemble the materials, and keep them in the designated area. Teachers who use this approach:

- Analyze the classroom to find a designated area for materials—closet, shelves, undershelf system.
- Empty the space.
- Possibly create shelves and/or make hanging storage systems.

Key to the particular place approach is that it is single purpose—for materials only, not squeezing materials into space already in use. A tote-it is also useful to bring materials from a particular place.

Your organization may be entirely different or some combination. The main points are for materials

- to be easily seen and reached,
- to be orderly,
- not to avalanche when you remove something,
- not to crumple, tear, or break,
- to be aesthetically pleasing.

Container Systems

Containers are essential for organization. If you have funds, you can purchase containers and build shelves that just fit them. My alternatives require little money. Containers make the difference between a collection of "stuff" and a storage *system*. Better to have many containers all the same than two of this and three of that. With cardboard boxes—from shoes, bulk crackers, chips, laundry soap, oatmeal—using just one type makes storage easier and provides a more pleasing aesthetic. Identical boxes stack and their graphics create a rhythm, both factors that make a system orderly. Glass jars are round, square, skinny, or squat. Using identical jars in a few heights or girths enables you to position shelving so the containers look orderly. Principles that apply to any container are: many, identical, stackable, and fit a particular space. The advantage of jars is being able to see what is inside, putting the emphasis on the material, not the container.

If you use opaque containers, fasten a sample on the exterior so you can remember what is inside. Inexpensive containers can be found at dollar, hardware, secondhand, or discount stores. Before shopping determine your budget so you don't waste time considering something too expensive. Follow the same principle for *found* containers—many identical in a limited size range rather than a few of these and those. Identical means exactly the same material, color, and shape; only size varies.

Once you have individual containers, they need space, which in time may need to expand. Stacking trays hold paper effectively. Tubes of paint are best out of reach! Storage systems are works-in-progress. A teacher with useless undercounter kitchen cupboards removed the door fronts, installed fluorescent tubes for each shelf, and hid the tubes behind translucent plexiglas. She installed the plexiglas leaving just enough shelf depth to hold a jar, and displayed materials in glass jars. The area glowed! The colors mesmerized. It became an aesthetic focal point in the room, drawing the children to the materials and heightening their awareness of the materials' categories and attributes.

Places to Work

The most important aspect of a work space is that you, the teacher, do not worry about it. If you fear a surface will be damaged or a floor stained, you will not relax. Choose spaces you can cover and clean easily. Floors, tables, counters, and desks are all suitable and over time you may use all for different activities. Questions to consider:

- Will the child be comfortable?
- Will material fit in the space?
- Is the chair seat the right height?
- Can the child move readily without tipping or falling off?
- Is there room for the adult to be comfortable too?
- If the surface or surfaces require protection, is there a reasonable way to do so?
- How accessible is water if you need to clean something quickly?
- Will the child be safe if the adult is diverted?
- If you need additional material during the activity, is there room nearby?
- Will you be able to continue the activity without someone else requiring the space?

CONCLUSION: MATERIALS' MEANING

Materials draw children like honey draws bees. When an adult uses materials with intention, they stimulate the senses and become the stuff for the exercise of "core knowledge" (Spelke & Kinzler, 2007). They are the stimulus to focus attention and foster maturational imperatives. They abound in homes and can be repurposed in numerous ways. Use of materials requires preparation, well worth the time because preparation frees you to concentrate on the child's reaction to the material. I call the introduction of a material "framing" and explain the related brain mechanisms and give examples in Chapter 2.

2

Framing Experiences

Movement is a fundamental basis of learning, because it is a major aspect of experience every second of every day . . . and is important for purely mental tasks.

—John Ratey (2002)

Picture: An 8- to 10-month-old baby holding a paintbrush sits in the cut-out center of a huge piece of paper. Jars of red, yellow, blue, and green paint are nearby, each with its own brush. She has painted many long strokes, possible because the paper extends far beyond her reach. This took place in a Reggio infant/toddler center. On my first visit to Reggio I became convinced that we wait far too long to introduce materials like tempera paint, glue, clay, mark-makers, and light and shadow to children under 3, and that we can offer infants/toddlers experiences hitherto introduced in preschool, kindergarten—or never.

Picture: Bertie, 24 months, did not yet speak much, but noted everything and used his hands with amazing precision. When a pair of tongs with a fork on one side and a spoon on the other appeared at the dinner table to serve the broccoli, he was riveted, pointed at them, and demanded: "Machine!" The five adults at the table understood that he wanted to use the tongs, handed them to him, and watched, astonished, as the toddler manipulated broccoli onto his plate. He managed to grip and wield the tongs like a pro on his first try. Teachers who believe in infant and toddler competence keep at-hand some tools that can pose a significant challenge.

In this chapter I explain what framing means and its relation to the brain and to infant/toddler competence. I use the practice of framing to introduce common materials and tools. Scenarios show beginnings—how to choose materials, introduce experiences, manipulate simple tools. My approach is didactic because I have observed teachers hesitant to use the tools or materials I describe and have seen teachers try similar activities but give up quickly, unsure of what or how to do something. Therefore, descriptions are precise. Make adjustments based on your comfort level and your infants and toddlers.

THE BRAIN'S ATTENTION SYSTEMS

Framing means taking control of the brain. We do this by alerting and sequencing. These actions help to build concentration.

Alerting

Framing an experience keeps the brain's reticular activation system alert. This is the part of the brain stem that receives input from most of the senses and from other parts of the brain. If the beginning of an activity is flat and mechanical, with limited meaning and without an arresting element, the brain feels a lack of activity. In many cases this induces a state of sleepiness, manifest as boredom (R. Feuerstein, lecture, 2007).

When and where a teacher does an activity, and whether she is free from distractions so she can concentrate, determines the activity's success. In introducing *any* material, teachers feel more at ease if they:

- choose a time they and the infant/toddler are least tired;
- choose a calm time;
- ignore distractions;
- decide whether to have a one-on-one or small-group experience;
- gather everything needed beforehand even if it means postponing the experience and using the time to organize;
- think through the activity in advance several times;
- rehearse the activity to learn how the materials behave;
- strategize how to encourage children to go beyond 2 minutes;
- act with intentionality by focusing eyes, head, posture, and attitude on the child.

Giving total attention—never turning your back on a child—is the best possible safety measure.

Sequencing

Framing involves breaking down the complex processes of activities into their separate parts (task analysis). This activates the brain's attention/consciousness reaction. To neuroscientists the word *attention* has a different meaning than its common use of serious noticing. It connotes an executive brain function with separate processes—ignoring some stimuli, juggling many, focusing and staying focused, ascribing an emotional tone to an experience. Four functions in the attention system enable the brain to "monitor" (Ratey, 2002, p. 115) the environment, the specific experience, the sequence of the experience, and the processes in the brain itself:

- Vigilance is controlled by the brainstem, the lowest level, so that we can remain attuned.

- Physical reorientation is controlled by the motor cortex, the next level, that alerts us to opportunities or threats in the environment.
- Detection of new or rewarding stimuli is controlled by the limbic system.
- Action, reaction, and integration of immediate and longer range goals are controlled by the frontal lobes in the cortex. (Ratey, 2002, pp. 114–115)

Sequencing with infants and toddlers builds the attention/consciousness functions in the brain. Throughout evolution, attention and consciousness have been essential for survival. They determine how successfully children navigate the complexities of modern-day life.

One way to decide how to sequence an activity is to analyze the complexity. For example, to open a door requires

- walking toward the doorknob,
- aiming your hand toward its mark,
- configuring your hand to the shape of the doorknob,
- gripping the knob tightly,
- deciding in which direction your hand must turn to disengage the latch,
- keeping the knob turned so the latch stays disengaged,
- pulling (or pushing) the door,
- releasing the latch when the door is open,
- removing your hand.

If you want to *sneak* into a room or keep from waking someone, you must disengage and release the latch so that you prevent it from making noise. Children in my Montessori class loved surprising one another by opening doors noiselessly.

Breaking down an activity helps children imitate. It is easier to learn any complex activity if separate actions are isolated and sequenced.

In sequencing, the brain must

- organize the logical order of the task or the information;
- integrate the information with what one already knows;
- retain the order over the time the task requires;
- reorganize the information within the brain so that it can be recalled and used later.

Memory, learning, and all kinds of thinking depend on these abilities (Ratey, 2002). Using *any* material requires mastering complex sequences—multiple actions each with many subroutines. Everyday actions that adults perform automatically are high-level challenges to young children—dressing, pouring, catching, and many more.

Building Concentration

The ability to concentrate is essential to learning anything. Several complex brain functions are required:

- Focus—directing your attention to what is at hand;
- Sustained attention—maintaining focus over time;
- Memory—keeping in mind the steps to complete the task;
- Sequencing—performing the steps in a logical order;
- Naming—labeling different parts of an activity with words.

If children select activities that interest them, they will be motivated, will attend, and thus will learn to concentrate. Children who concentrate are *in flow*, a mental state conducive to learning (Csikszentmihalyi, 1990). The sequence is: Interest begets focus; focus begets sustained attention; sustained attention begets concentration; concentration begets thinking. This works best if there is an intentional adult who observes and at pregnant moments provokes the child with well-targeted mediation. Mediating well is an art. Some teachers are natural mediators. Others can acquire mediation techniques.

FACING COMPLEXITY

Adults accomplish many complex tasks because they have habituated the subroutines in each. The more repeated experiences children have in the bits of actions that are the foundation for more complex actions, the more facilely they will think. Neuroscientists call repeated experience *training the brain*. Here we watch how to help children train their brain to frame an experience. We also see soliloquy, a technique to learn framing by using language; it is especially effective for children lacking rich language experiences. Finally, I discuss the process of habituating a skill.

Training in Framing

Jan thought making a collage might fascinate her 2-year-olds. She remembered that in last year's group some were bothered by feeling glue on their fingers, others intrigued by its stickiness. So, she decided to isolate the different processes in collage. Gluing became an experience unto itself. She prepared

- paper, dark but vividly colored, the size of half a sheet of copier paper
- four small bottles of Elmer's white glue

She chose four 20-month-olds who were usually open to new experiences. First the children watched as Jan pulled up the bottle top and riveted her attention on very carefully squeezing a drop of glue onto a piece of paper, building the children's desire to do it themselves. Then she gave each child a paper and a glue bottle. Twenty minutes later the four were still squeezing, touching, and smearing—exploring how glue behaves. Their rapt attention gave her feedback: Her decision to isolate gluing had been correct. Jan had the children glue some *thing* only when their fascination waned many weeks later. Even then, she occasionally used glue alone, or waited for children to ask to glue something. Glue alone is fascinating to toddlers around 14 to 28 months and to older children, especially if they have never experienced glue.

Sometimes children finish in a minute an activity you planned to engage them for 5 or 10 minutes. To slow down and make experiences last longer, Anita gathers materials with children rather than laying them out in advance. To three 24- to 28-month-olds: "While you were napping, I thought of some *great* materials! Would you like to *draw* today? Let's find the paper." After they find and lay out the paper: "Now choose some markers." When they finish, she reverses the process with them, putting everything away and, if the area is messy, cleaning it up. This parses a complex process—gather, lay out, do, put away, clean—into small bits. Children may spend more time gathering and cleaning up than on the activity itself. Gathering materials heightens anticipation and helps children learn where things are kept; cleaning up gives a sense that they are doing real work, like adults do. If gathering becomes tedious, Anita keeps a tray with materials at hand but out of sight until she is ready for them.

Delores teaches 2-year-olds. This is her initial presentation:

> When I introduce painting to children who have not had much experience with it, I lay the materials out beforehand. Otherwise the experience becomes the before and after steps. Only as the children grow more familiar with the material do I involve them in gathering and cleaning up. For me, gathering materials when something is first introduced makes working with the material itself feel unfocused. I introduce the materials and emphasize the vocabulary: "Now I am going to put *paint* on your *palette*. This is your *paintbrush*."

Delores is mediating meaning. Anita, who gathered the material with the children, has a different goal: to slow children down; Delores's goal is to emphasize material and vocabulary. Both teachers respect process and break activity into stages.

Elly, working with infants from 5 to 8 months, carefully lays out protective paper, painting paper, and paint. She puts three jars of paint, hues of one color, on a tray and unscrews the jar tops so infants reach in with their hands. She seats those who can sit and holds infants who cannot. Two children make marks all over the paper. Two others are more interested in exploring the paint on their hands.

Neuroscience recently has shown us that

> Motor activity takes place in three stages. First we analyze the incoming external and internal data. Next we formulate and monitor a response plan. Then, we execute the plan. The second stage, formulating and monitoring a response plan, is the step that involves thought-processing. Thinking is indeed a process, a biological function controlled by the brain. (Ratey, 2002, p. 176)

Thinking is a very complex process. To think, our brains

Painting challenges infants to use their body, and especially the eye/hand nexus, in new ways.

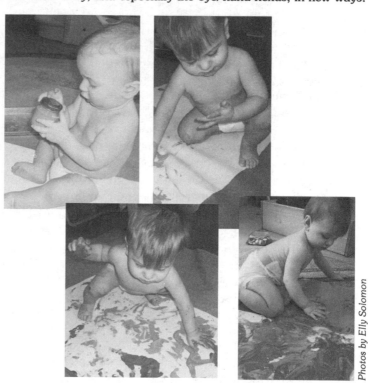

Photos by Elly Solomon

- receive,
- perceive,
- comprehend,
- store,
- manipulate,
- monitor,
- control, and
- respond

to stimuli that steadily change (Ratey, 2002, p. 176). The process involves

> a flow of signals between nerve cells . . . [particularly the] three major classes of neurons [brain cells]. . . . Sensory neurons . . . respond to a specific type of stimulus from the outside world . . . and send this information to the brain. Motor neurons . . . control the activity of [muscle and gland cells]. Interneurons, the most numerous class of neurons in the brain, serve as relays between sensory and motor neurons. (Kandel, 2006, p. 66)

You may feel your children will never use paint (or clay or collage). Then, voila! One day they become deeply engaged! You have taught them how to frame activities, not to rush in headlong, so they now stage complex activity for themselves.

Narrating an Experience

Some teachers keep up a running stream of words and talk about everything as they do it as a way to encourage children to think about the meaning of an activity. For example, while holding hands as they walk to where the painting materials are, Lauren says to her 2½-year-olds in a soliloquy: "Let's go get the paint. What color do you think it will be? (Listens to responses.) Will it be green like the grass or orange like the juicy fruit? (Listens to responses.) The paint is here on the cart. This is its *place*." As her children turn 3: "Something *crinkly* is on the shelf. What do you think it's made of?" She verbalizes for younger ones: "No, it's *not* fall leaves! No, it's *not* scrunched up newspaper. Yes! It *is* silver foil!" She is mediating meaning, using words to provide content because to think, you have to think about something. Content (red, yellow, orange) is the "stuff" of concepts (color), and children under 6 have, literally, a world of content and concepts to learn.

Other teachers find words distracting. The technique you choose depends on the children. Feuerstein calls the stream-of-words *soliloquy* and considers it essential for children who are non-English-speakers or from homes without language-rich environments (Feuerstein, Falik, & Feuerstein, in press).

Habituating Essential Skills

Adults take for granted the ability to make complex movements, handle tools, or bend materials to their purposes. But for children under 3 everything is new. Complex tasks may foil them if they cannot perform the simpler tasks that are embedded. For example, children must figure out how to open and close scissors before trying to use them to cut some*thing*. Experiences in this book are broken into manageable sequences: It is enough to make glue come out of a bottle, explore its texture, and learn how it behaves, before using it to make things stick.

Movement rivets infants' attention, and toddlers are fascinated by the challenge of making precise movements. In any complex procedure each movement involves a specific task for each joint, finger, hand, arm; for eyes, head, neck, torso. Because children under 3 are just learning how to synchronize parts of their body, isolating subroutines matters. The purpose for using materials is not to make children artists, bookbinders, or tailors, but to help them develop the coordination among lower level brain functions that must be established before they can engage in higher level thinking.

The word *lower* does not mean a less important function—just the opposite. Lower means essential: The ability to focus on stimuli, sustain attention, and discriminate salient features are three of a myriad of lower-level brain functions. They are the first functions the brain must master because more complex thinking/doing depends on them. Special educators know that children may fail to function and learn effectively because they haven't mastered these abilities. Using materials with toddlers under 3 provides numerous ways to activate, and varied ways to repeat, these functions *at an age when the brain is predisposed to do so* and the child is motivated by the novelty.

Repetition is essential to consolidate a skill, and variety is essential to keep the brain focused. Providing repetition with variety satisfies the brain's requirement for novelty. With repetition, complex processes become habituated so that eventually different areas of the brain function together automatically (Ratey, 2002). Variety makes repetition palatable and pleasurable.

CHALLENGES: GLUE, SCISSORS, CLAY, SEWING

Observe 8-month-olds' concentration as they grapple with the finger control needed to pull a glob of clay from a hunk. Revel with 20-month-olds as they experiment with the stickiness of glue. Wonder at a not-yet-3-year-old's theory-making: "At night the shadow goes up in the sky near its lamp" (Dolci, 2000, p. 30). Challenging activity is essential for brain development. The brain requires stimulation. Challenging activity, structured so children can master it, stimulates the brain. For toddlers, whose movements are imprecise, challenge focuses the brain and, when the challenge is met, motivates the child who knows she has mastered something complex. The following scenarios portray techniques for introducing challenging materials or tools.

Glue Sticks vs. Glue

Glue sticks leave traces that are hard for children to see and that smudge; thus they encourage imprecision. They also substitute an easier for a more complex process. Squeezing out a drop of glue, or even a stream, is a more challenging movement. The virtual replacement of glue with glue sticks is a symptom of a hurried-up culture. While glue sticks are fine while waiting in a restaurant or on an airplane, they cannot substitute for the skills required to use glue. These include:

- Eye coordination: What is the best angle to hold the bottle?
- Assessing quantity: How much is needed for this job?
- Precision: Where exactly do I want the glue?
- Hand skill: What is the right amount of pressure to make something stick?
- Judgment: Has the glue dried up?

Using glue requires the brain to analyze and be precise, and therefore challenges the brain.

Practical Life Activities

Each practical life activity, found in Montessori classes, has a particularly challenging part. Pouring exercises challenge children from around 20 or 24 to 36 months or more; they involve extreme concentration and precise control of both hands! Polishing requires turning your fingers into polishers by carefully folding

From before the age of 2 pouring is a highly engaging activity. This 21-month-old has been taught to handle a pitcher precisely so the liquid reaches its destination.

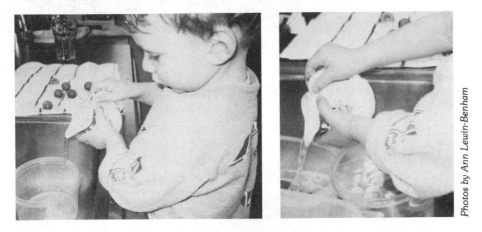

Photos by Ann Lewin-Benham

them inside a polishing cloth and holding the cloth firmly so it does not unwrap mid-job. Scrubbing a table has many challenges: using an *amount* of water that makes suds but does not slosh; rubbing *enough* soap from the cake onto the brush bristles so it lathers. Polishing metal includes a big challenge, making a polish applicator from an orange stick and ball of cotton. The movement: Jab the orange stick into the cotton ball just so and flick off enough cotton to wrap around the end of the stick. Some children manage the other movements in metal polishing, but bring stick and cotton to a teacher or friend to make the applicator. Then, one day the child makes his own! It provides a rush of endorphins, powerful chemicals that create the sense of well-being when you know you have mastered something difficult. Children thrive on challenge, are bored without it, and know the difference.

Scissors

Walt is an artist/teacher. His medium is cut paper, those extremely intricate designs sometimes found in stationers or exhibits. When his toddlers are around 14 months, he carefully chooses those who are calm enough and one-on-one introduces the skill of cutting. He uses round-tipped, metal-blade children's scissors (Fiskars and Crayola are good brands). Plastic blades would tear, not cut, the paper.

Walt demonstrates how to open and close the blades by using one hand to hold each side of the scissors handle. Then he helps the toddler hold one handle in her right hand and the other in her left, positions his hands over the toddler's, and opens and closes the blades with her. Each time he says, "Open," as the scissors open or "Close," as they close. Then he removes his hands and encourages the child to try on her own. He repeats this, with as much assistance as needed; then, right at her side, lets the child try herself. Walt finds 2 to 5 minutes a good amount of time; some children work as long as 10.

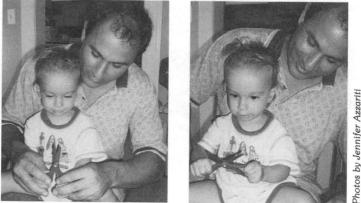

Opening and closing scissors rivets attention.

Photos by Jennifer Azzariti

When fascination with opening and closing wanes, Walt adds paper. Toddlers do not have the strength or dexterity to hold scissors correctly—thumb in the smaller hole, other fingers in the larger. Each time he begins, Walt arranges a toddler's fingers to provide the correct positioning, but encourages the toddler to open and close the scissors however she can until the necessary strength and control develop.

Scissors and Paper. Lisa says, "Once toddlers 'get' cutting, there is no stopping them." She watches for the time to cut some *thing*. For some toddlers it is almost as soon as they begin using scissors; for others it is months later. Lisa uses medium-weight paper such as cardstock or construction paper, cut into strips no wider than 1 inch and between 6 and 9 inches long. The weights and lengths are intentionally specific. If the paper is too flimsy or too thick, it will be difficult to cut. If the strips are too short, toddlers could cut their fingers. Approximately 1 inch is the maximum width a toddler can cut in one stroke. A wider piece is too challenging.

The goals are: cut off a snip of paper and learn the purpose for using scissors. Lisa says, "Open," and inserts a strip of paper into the blades as the toddler opens them. Then she asks the toddler to close the scissors and cut a piece off. A toddler may be having too much fun exploring the actions of opening and closing to wait for Lisa to insert the paper. If this happens, Lisa leaves paper for another day. Another toddler might be so fast that Lisa must move fast, sticking the paper in the instant the scissors open. When toddlers see that *their* action causes the result, they can't get enough! Lisa starts each session by showing the correct way to hold the scissors. At some point, maybe days or months later, toddlers hold the scissors correctly on their own. There is no right or wrong time.

When fascination with cutting snips of paper begins to wane, Lisa does something else with the paper. If a toddler is still attentive after a cutting session, she has him glue what he just snipped so he can see further purpose for his actions: "Remember yesterday (or last week) you cut these snips? Today we're going to *collage* them!"

Cutting snips of paper gives an 18-month-old the satisfaction of accomplishment.

Photos by Jennifer Azzariti

First Scissors Experiences. Lisa describes her first scissors experience:

I started cutting with Jerome when he was 14 months old. He had often watched me and other children cut and wanted to try himself. At first, he swiped closed blades across the paper strip, like cutting with a knife. I had to stick the paper into the blades quickly while they were open because he was too excited about the open/close action to wait. Later, when he understood the cause and effect of cutting, he would pause, waiting for me to put the paper strip between the blades. After about six experiences, he tried on his own to put his fingers in the scissors handle correctly, but still couldn't open them. About 3 months later, he could put a full sheet of paper, 8½ x 11", into the blades and cut across it. He would find paper and scissors himself and cut for a full 10 minutes.

At 24 months Henry was able to slightly open and close scissors with one hand, but had more control with two. He kept opening and closing the scissors until paper was inserted. At first he tried to swipe the paper with closed blades and was not open to suggestions. Then he made short cuts, opening the blades, but not closing them completely on the paper, sort of stabbing at the paper, trying to cut it by using the open blades and pushing. His results looked like fringe. A great result! A fine first experience!

However a toddler under 3 begins something new is fine. Do not expect the perfected action or outcome that adults associate with the process. Enjoy whatever the child attempts. An adult's enjoyment fosters a desire for more experience.

Gluing Paper

Wendy fully believes in the power of materials to engage toddlers in extended activity. She loves collage. She uses Elmer's glue, a 1.25 oz. bottle, finding that school glue does not work as well. Her base is cardstock or construction paper, about a 6- or 8-inch square or rectangle. She saves small pieces of paper, cut by the children, and lays them out on a small, shallow tray (solid-colored so a tray's pattern does not compete with the papers). She keeps a damp cloth at hand. To ensure an aesthetic experience, Wendy uses papers with an attractive back side because toddlers do not distinguish front and back. In other words, she avoids scrap paper that is junky on one side.

In her setup, Wendy places the base paper in front of the toddler and the bottle of glue to left or right, depending on whether hand preference is obvious. She experimented alone to find the right bottle opening so the glue drips without too much squeezing, but does not pour. She places the tray of papers within easy reach, a separate tray for each child.

Wendy begins: "*You* cut all these pieces of paper." (Or, "I cut all these pieces of paper for you.") "Would you like to use some glue and stick them on *here* (touching base piece)?" She invites them: "Squeeze a tiny drop of glue on the paper." On the first try some children do just a drop. Some toddlers continue to enjoy the glue alone. When their interest wanes or for others who are ready immediately, Wendy introduces the next step, offering a piece of cut paper as the child puts glue on the base paper: "Put this on top of the glue."

Most children catch on immediately. If not, Wendy encourages: "Would you like to put another piece of paper on the glue? The glue will make it stick." The process delights most children! When Wendy sees that children are finished, they wipe their fingers with the damp cloth, look at the collage together, and decide on a place for it to dry. Wendy always converses: "Now the glue needs to dry. Can you think of a safe place to put your collage while the glue is drying?" Later they revisit the collage: "See? The glue made the papers stick."

Some teachers find that glue tops stick or clog. Wendy kept the tops glue-free by wiping the spouts with a damp cloth and showing the children how to do this themselves. When necessary, she removed the tops and ran them under hot water. With children new to gluing, she kept bottles less than full.

Using liquid glue requires a 16-month-old to use judgment and precise hand skills.

Photos by Jennifer Azzariti

Throughout the experience, children smear glue, pour it in puddles, and pull off collaged pieces, all part of the process—and Wendy never discourages them: "Even toddlers who have used glue alone may still treat it as a material in and of itself and utilize its adhesive properties later." With gentle reminders that glue sticks objects together, children begin to see its purpose, although Wendy never subverts the delight in gluing by hurrying on to sticking. It may happen by accident and be a surprise. The experience differs for every child.

Clay

Stan begins to use clay with infants as soon as they can sit, around 6 to 8 months. He prefers white or terra cotta artists' clay (also called low-fire), not self-hardening clay. The white is less messy because the terra cotta color can adhere to skin and surfaces. It is available at local clay studios, art stores, or online, usually sold in 25-pound bags for about $11. Stan stores it in heavy, twist-tied plastic bags that he uses to line two large plastic containers with tight-fitting lids. One holds "working" clay, the other extra. So the clay won't stick to the table, he covers the table with canvas, available at art stores. (Masonite boards or heavy fabric also work.) Nearby are wire cutters (available from art suppliers or made from two short dowels for handles, wrapped with picture wire or dental floss). A spray bottle with water keeps the clay moist. An adult can make slabs with a full-size wooden rolling pin (a process beyond toddlers' ability).

A 25 pound block of clay lasts a long time when cared for. After working with clay, Stan gathers the pieces into a ball, sprays with a bit of water, and wedges them together as if he is kneading bread dough. To prevent mold Stan makes sure to remove materials (shells, sticks, buttons, beads), shake excess clay from the canvas, and hang it to dry before folding. If clay dries out, he punches holes in it with his fingers and adds water. He rehydrates rock-hard clay by soaking it in water, letting the excess evaporate, and air-drying until it reaches the desired consistency.

To help toddlers learn how clay behaves, Stan opens the *full* bag with them. "Clay comes from the earth [or ground or soil]." He asks them to feel it: "Is it warm or cool? Is it dry or moist?" Or, "The clay feels so warm. The clay is very moist." He encourages them to touch, poke, squeeze, pinch, and pound the clay as long as they are interested. He invites a very interested child to use the wire cutter. Holding the wooden handles, Stan wraps the wire around the back of the clay block and pulls toward the front, then lifts off the piece. Nan, a 10-month-old, was mesmerized. Most toddlers love helping pull the wire cutter, and when they can, Stan lets them cut alone, encouraging them to cut as much as they want. It is another of those fascinating actions, like making the polishing stick, that builds brain capacity through challenge. Because clay is dense and strong, Stan makes sure smaller pieces, which are easier to manipulate, are available. With children averse to touching clay, Stan says, "I'll play with it," and comments on his own movements or how the clay feels as he manipulates it. Or, he includes the child with a small group that enjoys using clay.

Sewing

Elizabeth loves embroidery herself, so invites toddlers around 2½ years to embroider. She uses a small embroidery hoop about 7 inches in diameter, blunt needles about 1½ inches long, and cotton thread, doubled and knotted, about 10 inches long; she always has several threaded needles ready since children make long stitches and use up thread quickly. She finds a needle threader helpful, and children readily learn to use this tool. Elizabeth uses open-weave fabric so the needle goes through easily and solid-colored fabric so the stitches are visible—dark fabric with light thread or vice versa. She cuts the fabric to fit the hoop so the overhang is not in the way of the sewing. For her own use when preparing materials, she keeps a fabric scissors, rotary cutter, and cutting mat nearby.

Children find the action of sewing fascinating. To begin, Elizabeth, one-on-one, child at her side, helps the child, to the extent possible, put the fabric on the hoop. She shows the child the front and back, threads one needle, and starting from the backside, demonstrates: "We start from the back so the knot won't show on the front." Using soliloquy, she talks through what she is doing: "I'm pulling the thread through until it stops. Then I go down again." After a few stitches she turns the material over to the child. At first *she* holds the hoop. Once he understands the technique, she lets the toddler hold it himself, making sure the hoop isn't flat in his lap so he won't sew the fabric onto his clothing (as I have done more than once!). Elizabeth's examples of toddlers' typical comments: "Watch, it's back uuup, and doooown, up and down, up and down. Oops! It's going to poke through my knee. See, it's going through the line. I did it. I think it's going to poke into the chair."

Elizabeth varies the activity by adding more thread colors and buttons, beads, shells, washers—anything with holes. She provides paper or clear acetate (as used with overhead projectors) to sew on. Later children can sew fabric pieces together, draw simple lines to follow with stitches, and sew on fringe, small scraps of fabric, tassels, or other trims.

2½-year-olds are fascinated by the up/down movement of a needle and the design that thread makes.

Photos by Jennifer Azzariti

CONCLUSION: ACCUMULATING SKILLS

Elliot Eisner (2002), who holds professorships in art and education at Stanford, says:

> For young children the sensory world is a source of satisfaction, and imagination [is] a source of exploratory delight. And it is these inclinations toward satisfaction and exploration that enlightened educators and parents wish to sustain rather than to have dry up under the relentless impact of "serious" academic schooling. A culture populated by a people whose imagination is impoverished has a static future. (p. 5)

The approach and experiences described in this chapter can be adapted to introduce anything new. The framework is the same for any activity. Chapter 3 focuses on infants, then seven chapters each present a material that has endless possibilities, techniques specific unto itself, challenges, and limitless aesthetic potential. Such experiences stimulate a developing brain by training toddlers' attention and sequencing capabilities, all while refining the sensory and movement systems, cultivating the imagination, and building competence.

A left-brain/right-brain disjunction, all the rage in the 1980s, has been replaced by deeper understanding of the relation between the two hemispheres. While the right brain meanders and patterns, the left brain supplies and coordinates movement and language into expressive acts such as speech, writing, dance, or song. There are myriad forms of human expression that are understandable by others. Every single one of them "require[s] fine-motor movements" (Ratey, 2002, pp. 205–206).

Misbehavior often stems from boredom. By introducing materials, you change the state of a brain. Watch toddlers' eyes widen as you demonstrate something novel or challenging. As you train the brain to coordinate its different systems, you enable toddlers to undertake complex activity. Complexity trumps boredom! Once engaged in complex experiences, children focus, concentrate, thrive, and become competent.

Alexandra Cruickshank, who teaches children under 3, has the last word:

> We talk about slowing down, allowing time to explore a material, postponing an activity until you, the teacher, are ready. But in our product-oriented society, teachers often find themselves hoping for a product. We forget about slowing down and really allowing the children to experience the steps it takes to make something happen. For me the gradual accumulation of skills that show children's increasing competence is the most important.

3

Infants and Materials

The infant emerges as a remarkably well-programmed organism.
—Howard Gardner (1991)

Scenario: On the infant's feeding tray the teacher puts a rattle—vibrantly colored, easy to grasp, distinct noticeable sound. It simultaneously engages eyes, tactile sense, hearing, hand movement, and proprioception, the brain's understanding of where the body or limbs are in space. The infant grasps the rattle, hears the noise, releases its hand (at first accidentally), watches—intent as the rattle falls, surprised as it ceases to move on hitting the floor. The adult puts the rattle back on the tray and the infant, pleased by the complexity of the experience and the effect of her action, immediately repeats—grasp, release, drop, observe—listening to the rattling, soon learning to anticipate the "thud." If the infant could talk, she might say, "Go ump!" imitating the rattle hitting the carpet. She has invented a game, engaged in a science experiment, and experienced gravity—a big moment. Her teacher, by selecting the rattle and playing along enthusiastically, encouraged the exploratory behavior.

Adults trust they will remain with feet on the ground and not float off into space or continue to rise if they jump, because, as infants, they practiced dropping things, an experience that, literally, put the world in place. As infants engage in complex activities for long times, they form powerful ideas about how the world works. Educators "have not appreciated the strength of the initial conceptions, stereotypes, and 'scripts' [learned before age 5] that children bring to their school learning nor the difficulty of refashioning or eradicating them" (Gardner, 1991, p. 5).

We know a lot about infant perception, that almost from birth they can "distinguish an astonishing ensemble of forms, shapes, and line configurations" (Gardner, 1991, p. 45). Rochel Gelman and Elizabeth Spelke have done pioneering research on all aspects of infant perception, both devising reliable ways to observe infant cognition and conducting numerous studies. Because of their work we know that infants recognize visual or auditory patterns and have ideas about numerical processes. They have shown that infants perceive the same continuum of colors and sounds as adults, match objects they see to objects they feel, recognize faces, have "conversations," and separate animate and inanimate objects (Carey & Gelman,

40

1991; Gelman & Au, 1996; Gelman & Shatz, 1977; Mix, Huttenlocher, & Levine, 2002; Spelke, 1985, 1990, 1998; Starkey, Spelke, & Gelman, 1990).

This chapter has two themes: *infants' predispositions*, for example, learning through reciprocity or repetition, and *adults' intentionality*.

INFANTS' PREDISPOSITIONS

Many researchers note that infants are "pretuned" for social engagement or reciprocity, that almost from birth, infants are primed to seek and enjoy social interchange, even extended games (Feuerstein et al., 2006; Gardner, 1991; Gelman & Au, 1996; Mix et al., 2002; Spelke & Kinzler, 2007). They repeat actions over and over; repetition is another strong drive that is central to brain function. Here I discuss reciprocity and movement and their relation to repetition.

Reciprocity

In highly reciprocal interactions, adults offer and infants respond (or do not). Or, infants offer and adults respond. The dynamics of offer/response are what psychologists call reciprocity. Much of it is nonverbal. Semiotics theoretician Tom Sebiok says that over 98% of human communication is nonverbal. Infants stick their tongue out, following maturational imperatives to imitate and to move. They take about a year to develop the physical apparatus of speech, but can engage in conversation almost from birth. It is evidence of the deep-seated drive for social engagement.

Movement. Sara, an infant teacher, tapped into what Gardner (1991) calls the "predominantly ritualistic flavor [of interchange]" (p. 50) with 3-week-old Todd. She supported him with both arms, head cradled in her hands, his face about a foot from hers. Slowly and with great intention she stuck out her tongue. Todd immediately stuck his out. Sara sucked in her tongue; Todd sucked in his. Back and forth, adult and infant playing a game: my tongue out, yours out; mine in, yours in. After several minutes, a long time for a newborn, Todd turned his head aside, a cue he had had enough (Beebe et al., 1988). Two days later Sara held Todd in the same position. Immediately he stuck out his tongue! And the game continued.

Conversation. My grandniece, Zen, age 5½ weeks, seemed fussy, so I fed and changed her and then put her in her crib, no longer fussy but with no sign of sleepiness, just making typical, random, newborn movements. Then she made a random noise. I responded instantly, highly intentional, dramatic: "What a *beautiful* conversation. What *else* do you have to say?" then immediately stopped talking, focusing my entire being on her, while silence hung palpably. Zen worked hard, face and body straining for what felt like an eternity. Then, another random noise! Immediately I answered, same words, intentionality, and emotion. Again, Zen concentrated her entire being, trying to make a noise, the drive for social engagement compelling her to figure out what parts of her body made noise and how to use them. Gradually intervals between Zen's vocalizations and my responses lessened, eventually paced like a typical conversation. We were engaged in highly reciprocal activity. Had Zen wavered, become distracted, or turned away, I would have stopped. The conversation continued for more than 20 minutes.

These scenarios exemplify reciprocal activity. In normal infants, reciprocal games are joyful extensions of the tendency toward social interchange and favorably dispose infants to future interaction. Psychologist Reuven Feuerstein says reciprocity is both the need for someone to respond and the expectation that he will. Gardner calls such moments *potent*. "From the moment of conception . . . intimate and caring relationships are the fundamental mediators of successful human adaptation" (Shonkoff & Phillips, 2000, p. 27). Research agrees that lack of such bonds, especially not having them with a primary caregiver, has a negative and "major impact on . . . [young children's] cognitive, linguistic, emotional, social and moral development" (Shonkoff & Phillips, 2000, p. 341). In atypically functioning infants, adult stimulation of reciprocal action is essential, even therapeutic.

Repetition

Wiring the brain, the pastime of infants, requires repetition. Infants have seemingly endless capacity to repeat—dropping, banging, mouthing. Materials' properties are powerful stimulants; infants are drawn by:

- Appearance—size, shape, color;
- Behavior—falling, bouncing, rolling, wiggling;
- Sound—clangs, squeaks, is musical;
- Texture—squishes, scratches, is silky;
- Taste—cold, metallic, sweet.

With materials as their stimuli and props and repetition as their *modus operandi*, infants literally unravel the essence of how their world works. The scenarios later in the chapter describe experienced teachers who, bringing their own passions to an interaction, use readily available materials to encourage repetition. Each taps different maturational imperatives in the infant brain. Scenarios show one-on-one, not group, activity in order to emphasize salient features of the interchange.

Were we looking at Reggio classrooms, we would see mostly social activity. Reggio teachers place infants in close proximity to one another so that from the earliest months they can tap into social imperatives: the drives to be with, see, hear, and interact with other humans that result in imitation, adaptation, and growth. "Brain circuits are created and strengthened, in part, by whatever environment and experiences the baby encounters. The cellular architecture of the brain is changed through environmental exposure and experience" (Chugani, 2004, p. 2).

ADULTS' INTENTIONALITY

Adult intention is a primary force in children's learning (Feuerstein et al., 2006). Here we see teachers' intentionally building infants' awareness of language and emotion. In every interchange, there is a cycle of observation/provocation: Adults observe something an infant does and shape their response so that it provokes the infant to continue, as Zen's vocalization suggested conversing. Reggio teachers have honed observation/provocation to an art form. Observation is the prelude to the activities that follow; the teachers I describe are practiced at studying the nuances of infant behavior as the basis for their responses.

Using Language Intentionally

Kathy is outgoing and loquacious; her personality shapes the language games she plays. She particularly loves poetry, T. S. Elliot being among her favorites. Kathy holds infants in her arms and rocks them to cadences of poems in *Old Possum's Book of Practical Cats*. Words like *terpsicordian* roll off her tongue; rap-like rhythms of Jellicle Cats accompany her bouncing a baby. As they near 6 months, infants quiver when Kathy approaches, anticipating language, physicality, and closeness. Kathy also talks to infants about whatever they are doing: "What a good sleep you had. I'm getting you up from your nap now. *You're* ready for a diaper change and a *looong* drink of warm milk." Her patter marks every interchange. She varies tone of voice and inflections—whispering, emphasizing, drawing out syllables.

Pinker (1994) calls such talk "motherese":

- attracting babies' attention;
- enabling them to distinguish human speech from other noises;
- underscoring the difference between statements, questions, and directions;
- making sentence boundaries obvious;
- helping infants notice new words. (p. 284)

Kathy chooses *big* words, knowing that the brain's language systems thrive on hearing a great richness of language with clear pronunciation, full sentences, and varied vocabulary. She uses words like *slick*, *crunchy*, *fuzzy*, *tingly*, *warm*, and *shiny*, choosing adjectives from the many thousands in the English language.

Using Emotion Intentionally

Jeff is a person who naturally reads others. He notices infants' every nuance: sensitivity to noise, attempts to engage others, their ups and downs. He responds to infants with exaggerated reactions like surprise, wonder, or amusement—hamming it up regularly, acting astonished, feigning sadness, widening eyes, raising eyebrows, breathing deeply, grinning broadly, laughing open-mouthedly, puckering lips, wrinkling nose. His face expresses a full range of human reactions. Infants' imitations egg Jeff on as they play on their own emotional stage. Jeff also understands the power of body language and exaggerates his movements—pausing before beginning, hesitating a fraction of a second between distinct movements in a single gesture. He leans toward the infant, looks in her eyes, maintains total focus. The infant responds with increased movement, smiling, waving arms, kicking legs, quivering.

These teachers bring who they are to their interactions. What each loves, becomes the vehicle for interacting with an infant, suggesting the *mode* of a provocation—for Kathy language, for Jeff movement, especially facial expression. Each interaction is carried out with intention, is packed with meaning, and communicates *joy*. Kathy and Jeff choose times to play with infants when they are not pressured to do other things.

These teachers are also thoughtful documenters. They:

- Time how long infants remain interested.
- Keep records of date, number of repetitions, and length of game to look for patterns in infants' activity.
- Keep notes on infants' facial expressions, sounds, gestures, and other behaviors.
- Photograph or video record the infants.
- Record time of day, where the session occurred, and whether it was pre- or post-meal or -nap.

They think of themselves as researchers—observing, recording, comparing, predicting. They do so in order to more deeply consider the meaning of infant behavior and how their own responses can better foster maturational imperatives. Their records provide families with invaluable pictures of children's earliest months and become a body of evidence about infant development and a handbook of teacher innovations.

FOOD, PAPER, FABRIC, SOUND

The following scenarios show experienced teachers using food, paper, fabric, and sound with infants. Picture each scenario as a small group of infants. Small groups encourage social engagement as infants watch, listen, and move toward one another. Throughout each experience the mirror neurons—the clusters of synapses that are active when we see or hear—are firing. The mirror neurons are responsible for imitation, action that wires the brain (Gallese, Fadiga, Fogassi, & Rizzolatti, 1996).

Food

Cooking triggers Amanda's memories of her grandmother's pungent kitchen. She engages infants in numerous activities that vary with the season's produce or the whims of a bread-baking friend. An experienced teacher and a foodie, Amanda organizes food experiences for infants by smell—apples' or bananas' ripe sweetness; oranges' and lemons' pungency; cinnamon's, basil's, or rosemary's zest; fresh baked bread's sugar/yeast aroma; gingersnaps' or spaghetti sauce's complexity. She knows how long to heat foods to release their aroma. She never tires of watching an infant's eyes widen the first time she waves an orange segment under its nose. Janice, in the next classroom, triggers similar responses by using aromatic candles, perfumes, after-shave lotions, cakes of soap, and scents of grape hyacinth, roses, lily-of-the valley, or honeysuckle. (Caution: *No one* should smell anything powdery or granular.)

Both teachers use imitation, an innate brain response, and a primary means of learning. So Amanda brings the orange to *her* nose, holds it there, inhales deeply, registering surprise, knowing it will smell *very* intense to an infant. She breaks into a slow, rapturous smile letting feelings of pleasure overwhelm the feeling of surprise. In her "bag" of teaching tricks is expressiveness. She practiced before a mirror until she could easily show amazement, satisfaction, and pleasure. When Amanda offers the orange, she helps the infant cup his hands, places the orange into his "cup," and continues as necessary to help him bring hands to nose. With very young infants, Amanda holds the orange for them. She soliloquizes: "The orange smells pungent." Or: "Mmmmm, how orangey this smells!" Her favorite field trip is taking two or three infants to the grocery store and watching their responses to the different smells. After infants have had a range of experiences, Amanda presents two foods with contrasting odors—spicy and subtle—using the contrast to heighten their awareness.

Taste is underexploited as a way to stimulate mirror neurons. Alison helps infants taste food, not to stretch their palate, but so taste will trigger the formation of new networks of neurons. Her Taste Chart includes:

- applesauce
- bananas
- bran flakes
- cheerios
- lemon

The first sight, smell, and taste of an orange at 4 months alerts several senses simultaneously.

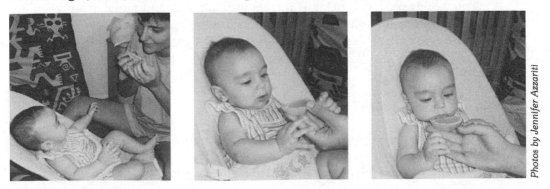

Photos by Jennifer Azzariti

- muffin, crumbly
- oatmeal
- peach—ripe, sweet, and peeled, or canned
- pudding, smooth
- orange segment
- fruit sherbet
- strawberries
- toast, hard

Alison follows a procedure. She puts three or four bran flakes within reach and, as the infant puts one in her mouth, provides words: "The bran flake feels crunchy." After the baby tires of bran flakes, she changes: "Cheerios seem to *dissolve* in your mouth." Eventually, she offers a contrast and enlarges vocabulary, using words such as *not*, *different*, or *same* to characterize an infant's choice. A bit of hard toast contrasts with a bit of crumbly muffin; a bit of applesauce, "bumpy and soft," with a bit of peach (peeled), "smooth and soft." Once an infant is familiar with different foods, there are many contrasts: textures of oatmeal and pudding; tastes of strawberry and lemon; feel of soy butter (a smidgen), "sticky, swallow hard," and sherbet, "smooth, slides right down." Alison never assumes a taste is too strong. Bertie, 11 months, loved to suck lemons. Danny, 18 months, ate all the gherkins on the condiment plate; Michael, 22 months, consumed black (pitted) olives by the canful.

Every family has its own food preferences—ethnic, vegetarian, bland, home-cooked, natural sugar, no sugar. Parents have different ideas about when to offer specific foods. Alison follows her families' preferences, skipping food tasting if it makes parents uncomfortable.

Paper and Fabric

Joan dabbles in mixed media as a hobby so has experience using a wide range of materials. She is particularly sensitive to the capacity of the hand to *know* through touch. Joan awakens infants' interest in materials with different varieties of papers and fabrics over many months:

- waxed paper
- copier paper
- silver foil
- colorful gift wrap
- velvet
- netting
- silk
- thick corduroy
- felt
- flannel
- wool
- cellophane

The 4-month-old is excited by the reflective foil and astonished as his mother's face disappears behind it, then reappears.

Photos by Jennifer Azzariti

She holds a sample about the size of a sheet of typing paper by two adjacent corners with index fingers and thumbs, slowly draws it over her face from top to bottom or, on another day, from bottom to top or side to side. She registers surprise as the material approaches her eyes and delight or amazement as her face is revealed. Then, using rich, descriptive vocabulary, she draws it slowly over the baby's face: "The silver foil feels slick" (or "smooth" or "cold"). "The waxed paper is translucent." Jonathan, 18 weeks old, played with the silver foil for almost 5 minutes, totally engaged, excitement obvious in his concentration, quivering, hard breathing, and leg kicking.

Joan crumples material into a ball (or if it won't crumple, rolls and ties it). She shows the infant how to hold and feel it all over: "The paper is crinkly." "The paper feels crumpled." "There seem to be so many edges." "The wool is bulky." "The netting feels stiff." Other times she explores the material *with* the infant, guiding the infant's hands as necessary to feel it all over, push it tighter, pull it apart, poke with one or several fingers, pinch, or squeeze.

When infants show interest in a particular movement or material, Joan repeats it at the next session, introducing something new only after interest wanes. With exploratory infants who try movements on their own or quickly go through a range of movements, Joan spends a long time herself on a single movement, wondering: "This thick wool won't stay crumpled!" Laughing: "It keeps bouncing back to its original shape! Isn't that *funny*?" She models the possibilities and surprises in lengthy engagement because one of her intentions is to help infants sustain their attention. Her sense of timing is good, not interrupting if an infant is engaged but commenting on an outcome or chuckling at results to stretch an infant's attention.

With oral infants, Joan exclaims with a disgusted facial expression: "Yuk! Paper is a *terrible* thing to eat." Registering extreme pleasure she quickly substitutes a toy suitable for mouthing: "This rattle is *lovely* to chew." With extremely oral infants, she uses only items suitable for mouthing.

Joan sees the world as an endless wealth of materials to explore:

- books
- clothing
- jars
- pans
- spoons
- stuffed animals
- wooden objects
- small brushes

Sometimes Joan rubs an item gently on her cheek, registering surprise: "This book feels *hard*." Or, "This jar feels *cold*." Then, she rubs the item gently on the infant's cheek: "Can you feel how *hard* the book is?" ("how soft the shirt feels?" "how fuzzy the wool?" "how smooth the wood?")

Sound

Chandra finds in sound the same wealth that Alison finds in food, and is committed to exploring all aspects of sound. She uses many common items, two of each, that sound different when touched, banged, clapped, or shaken:

- spoons, metal and wooden
- discarded CDs
- wooden blocks
- rhythm instruments, particularly small drum, tambourine, "egg" shakers, castanets, wooden sticks (dowels cut to about 6", ends sanded)
- opaque containers like old film canisters (tip: roll dark paper in pill bottles to make them opaque; glue tops securely), which she uses for matching games, partly filling each pair with one of the following, labeling the bottom to identify contents:
  - rice
  - lentils
  - dried peas
  - lima beans
  - sand
  - salt
  - largish pebbles
  - pea gravel

Chandra encourages infants to bang. She begins with a pair of metal spoons (a wooden pair nearby and out of sight), holds them by the handle, gently hits the bowls together, and looks surprised at the noise: "What a clanging noise metal spoons make." She offers them to the infant, or places one in each of the infant's fists, providing whatever help is needed to grasp and clang them together. After several minutes, she quickly substitutes the wooden spoons, looks extremely surprised, cocks her head, and closes her eyes, emphasizing that she is listening intently: "What a clacking noise the wooden spoons make!" As the infant bangs, she comments on the quality of the noise: "Wooden spoons make a clackety sound." Back and forth, wooden to metal, for as long as the infant experiences pleasure in the action and noise.

Chandra shakes one of each sound container next to each ear, listening carefully, not saying a word, then stops shaking and whispers, "What a quiet sound rice makes." Or, "The rice sounds like the pitter patter of rain." If infants can, she helps them shake one container next to each ear, or encourages them to shake them however they can, or shakes the containers for an infant, each time listening intently, as long as the infant is interested. Then she comments on the sound.

If an infant tires quickly, Chandra introduces a pair of containers with a different sound, like pebbles, shaking it first herself: "The pebbles sound much *louder* than the rice." Then, she gives the containers to the infant (or shakes them for him), listening intently: "Pebbles make a rattley sound." The infant's interest determines whether she introduces a third pair.

Chandra plays castanets by holding one side in each hand and hitting them together, again listening closely, saying when finished: "Castanets make a clicking sound" or "add *rhythm* to music." She helps infants hold them, spoons nearby in case castanets are too difficult. She never pursues an activity that frustrates an infant, believing that enjoyment is essential and knowing there is no timetable because infants differ markedly in what captures their attention or when they can make an action.

Chandra plays a variety of CDs and also plays piano and guitar. She talks to infants about the feeling of different instruments and music—timbre, tempo, rhythm, mode. Don Campbell's book, *The Mozart Effect for Children* (2000), is inspiring and well informed. It suggests specific music for different ages, beginning in utero. Because music arouses strong feelings, it is an excellent "material" to use words that describe emotion—sad, moody, joyful, giddy, pensive—and matching facial expressions.

DAY BY DAY IN PROVOCATIVE INFANT SPACES

A series of photographs from a Reggio infant/toddler center shows a 10-month-old fascinated by a magazine page of wristwatches. The teacher places her wrist next to the infant's ear so the infant can hear her watch. The infant's eyes widen in surprise as she listens to the ticking. Then the infant puts her ear to the page to see if the pictures tick. The series shows that infants recognize that a picture represents an actual object and that infants have theories: If this watch ticks, the magazine picture might. It also shows the teacher's reciprocal actions, responding to an infant's cues second by second.

Environment-Richness

A prepared environment and its furnishings provide many experiences. The environment may include:

- light table
- mirrors
- climbing structure(s) or mats
- mirrored kaleidoscope
- overhead projector
- full-length, door-sized transparent panel

Monique places infants in front of a good-quality, unframed, securely mounted plexiglas mirror: "That's *you!*" Or, "Look at this fine (boy D'Antonio/girl Shameka) in the mirror!" Monique sits on one side of a transparent panel, infant on the other, playing games through the plexiglas. In Reggio schools mirrors are securely suspended over the diaper changing area, parallel (and out of reach) so infants see their reflection.

Material-Richness

The following list suggests materials that stimulate infants visually. Some are a permanent part of the environment, others used occasionally or rotated to renew interest:

- air-activated objects, generally inexpensive—balloons, some kites, colorful plastic spirals or twists
- lights
- magazines
- mobiles
- well-illustrated books, fiction and nonfiction
- sturdy cardboard tubes, all diameters and lengths
- transparent containers, empty or with a few choice objects

Lights are fascinating and comforting. From about 4 to 12 months many infants stare fixedly at a ceiling light or lamp, especially if it has an interesting feature. My dining area had a highly polished brass sunburst. Danny stared at it endlessly, vocalizing, waving his arms, quivering in excitement. Simply turning a light on and off stimulates the visual system. If an infant does not spontaneously notice, call her attention by pointing at it (see Chapter 1). Wonder-full, inexpensive lamps, under $20, are available at drug stores: 1950s lava lamps, fiber-optic sprays with color at the tips, plexiglas domes that change color. A collection can be rotated so infants have something new to look at. Cautions: *Never* use a strobe lamp; the rhythmic pulsing can trigger epilepsy. Be sure cords are out of reach and electric outlets have safety caps.

Infants use both hands and feet to move large lightweight objects.

Photo by Elly Solomon

Mobiles with clear, bright images, strong colors, and patterns with high contrast are best because the visual system is incapable of seeing pale colors and fine detail before about 3 months. Monique made mobiles for infants under 3 months with reflective and shiny objects, and for infants over 3 months with large photos of family or companions, faces hung parallel to the infants' faces.

Monique also uses inexpensive air-activated items in bright or iridescent colors—strips of plastic, cellophane, nested geometric shapes, kites. She plugs in a small whisper fan to make a slight breeze. She engages the infant's eyes: "Watch how quickly the strip spins." Or, "Look! The plastic reflects the sun." Or, "Watch the shapes turn in the breeze." Sometimes she turns the fan off and on, the stop/start of the mobile arresting the infant's attention. The fan's stream of air, falling on bare skin, provides the infant with a surprising tactile sensation.

For infants from birth or 3 months to about 12 months, repeated experiences smelling, touching, hearing, tasting, and seeing over many months heighten awareness of the environment, hone the senses, and activate different brain systems. They build the neural connections on which thinking depends. This overlaps with the time when infants can begin to use materials like tempera, glue, clay, paper, and natural and found objects, subjects of other chapters.

Five Months of New Materials

Using the Daily Journal prepared by teachers for parents, I tracked the introduction of new materials over 5 months in an infant room at the World Bank Children's Center in Washington, DC. In September the seven infants ranged from 1 month to 6 months. Note: *Many other things went on simultaneously in addition to what I describe.* My account focuses only on the *first time* a material is presented, not on the engagement of small groups of infants or the provocations with which teachers build on prior experiences and stimulate future experiences.

September 9: Music and Sound. Tracy (music teacher) sang in English and Chinese; played egg shakers, bells, tambourines, and a leather strap with bells; and floated scarves around the infants for about 1 hour.

September 12: Textures. The teachers used soft blocks (12" and under in height or diameter) and 6-inch square carpet pieces for infants to move toward, grasp, and handle.

September 16: Sensory Bottles. Teachers showed, shook, and encouraged infants to hold six to eight different-sized transparent plastic bottles filled with colored water, colored objects, or objects that make varied sounds.

September 18: Huge White Paper. Infants' attention was powerfully drawn to the sound of changing paper torn off the diaper table. Teachers "blanketed" infants in the paper, gave them crumpled balls of it, and encouraged them to roll or move through a mound of it.

September 23: Textures. Teachers offered wooden bowls and blocks, prominently ridged corrugated cardboard, and slick glossy paper, and helped infants rub their fingers over each.

September 25: Bubbles. Infants watched as teachers blew bubbles.

September 29: Reflective Materials. Teachers placed two infants in a cardboard rectangle lined with plexiglas mirror and open on both ends. They placed reflective found objects and CDs within reach.

October 2: Toys. Teachers provided small to medium-sized stuffed toys and stacking fabric rings for infants to move toward or grasp.

October 3: Sound-Makers. Tracy brought a small standing drum, rain stick, basket of blocks, and clackety caterpillar (toy from home). She "played" them and offered them to the infants to "play," helping them hold and move them.

October 7: Contrasting Papers. Teachers lowered over the infants and encouraged them to handle sheets of red cellophane and a handmade type of paper, red, soft, and easily crinkled.

October 22: Train Whistle. Tracy added a train whistle to the listening/playing experiences.

October 27: Interactions. Teachers put two infants side by side with a length of crumpled brown paper between them to encourage them to interact with the object and each other.

October 28: Textures. Teachers brought:

- a feather duster,
- empty tissue boxes, one filled with corks, one with leaves, and

- baskets, one with copper, another with plastic elbows and short lengths of pipe

for infants to handle, hold, drop, bang.

October 31: Transparency. [The classroom contains a light table 6" high x 24" square to pull up at or crawl on.] Differently colored transparent plastic drew infants to the light table to look through or crawl on the material.

November 4: Paper. Large waxy dots on a huge sheet of homemade-type paper encouraged feeling, crumpling, and crunching.

November 5: Music. The infants stared intently as Tracy danced for them.

November 6: Textures. Small, circular glass and metal containers were on the light table to be grasped, mouthed, rolled, dropped, or banged.

November 10: Books. Teachers read to two or three infants from a book with textures on each page and encouraged them to feel the textures, sometimes moving the infants' hands in a stroking or patting motion.

November 12: Movement. Several 18-inch lightweight plexiglas mirrored, faceted squares [lighting supply material] were brought for infants to crawl on, push, tilt, lift, taste, or wave.

November 17: Light. The light of an incandescent lamp reflected in a mirror stimulated moving toward, patting, and other interactions with the image.

November 18: Sounds. On the floor the teachers placed a huge ball of crumpled brown paper, bells with long handles, a xylophone, and maracas to reach for, roll on, or grab.

November 19: Sensory Experience. While music played, Tracy rhythmically lowered and raised a huge multicolored parachute in the middle of the group of infants.

November 20: Books. Teachers placed baskets of assorted board books on the floor for infants to turn over, grab, and examine.

November 24: Visual Stimulation. A new mobile made from lengths of colored plastic tube [fluorescent bulb covers] and connected by plumbing "Ls" was placed where the form encouraged infants to stare at its complex, sculptural shape.

December 4: Movement. Waxed paper stuffed inside a long, 4-inch diameter cardboard tube stimulated reaching, grasping, and pulling.

December 5: Movement/Vision. Teachers played peek-a-boo through long cardboard tubes.

December 8: Movement. Infants were given a basket with several of the classic baby toy "Skwish," available online (see Appendix A).

December 9: Hands. Baskets with different sensory items—rope, heavy sand-filled burlap, velvet with dry beans—encouraged grabbing, squeezing, dropping, and reaching.

December 10: Listening/Hands. Baskets with noise makers—sleigh bells and egg shakers—were placed within infants' reach.

December 15: Tactility. Transparent plastic bottles with corks, 2½-feet-square thick cardboard boxes, and a large soft doll encouraged infants to reach for, grasp, pull, tip, or shake.

December 18: Movement. With infants now more mobile, teachers play with them on the stairs and ramp to the loft.

January 8: Hands. Long, transparent Lego pieces on the light table provide a new impetus to configure fingers to grasp, push, and slide an object.

January 12: Hand/Eye. A bubble wand and a mirror toy in a hexagonal frame (see Appendix A) stimulate arm/hand/eye connections.

January 14: Movement. Long, large black cardboard tubes stimulate infants to reach for, move to, grasp, roll, or pile.

January 15: Light. Black felt and black paper with regularly spaced small holes to cover (or uncover) the surface of the light table stimulate infants to look at, swipe, or push.

January 22: Light/Shadow. Poster board with flaps allows light from the table to glow when the infants lift the flaps. Bubble wrap, rough different-colored papers, and thin papers, all light table sized, encourage new explorations of the light table.

January 26: Light/Shadow. Ridged, heavy-weight clear plastic, light table sized, encourages more exploration.

January 29: Light. A new light bulb in the fish tank renews interest.

January 30: Hands. Elly, the studio teacher, brought four infants to the Studio to use clay.

CONCLUSION: NATURAL LEARNERS

So, 5 months pass as infants notice, grasp, pull, roll, mouth, poke, stroke, and enlarge their capacities to handle and relate to materials, one another, and their teachers, all the while fulfilling maturational imperatives to move, repeat, imitate, socialize, and absorb language. "Babies' brains are wired to help them understand things about language, numbers, space, objects, and people—well before they can be taught this knowledge. . . . [These] learning-related skills are [important] in helping children succeed now and in the future, and . . . [all] involve executive functions of the brain" (Galinsky, 2010). The kinds of explorations described here motivate infants to continue and increase their engagement as natural learners.

4

Man-Made
Materials

The artist speaks to our capacity . . . for delight and wonder.
—Joseph Conrad (1897)

When you collect materials, you search with senses on edge: What glistens, what crunches, what feels cold to the tongue or soft to the fingers, what pulls, snaps, stretches, tangles, rolls, chimes? What is perforated so fingers can probe? What is pungent so the nose is alerted? What will make a body move differently? You look at everything as if you have never seen shapes, felt metal, shaken a jar of beans, or walked on ice. You search for materials that will bring the world to infants' and toddlers' senses: the nuances of 100 shades of green, the range of sounds the human ear can hear, the irregularities on a seemingly smooth surface. You seek for the uniqueness in each material and bring a world of essences into the classroom.

Each infant and toddler approaches material in his own way. One embraces, one engulfs, another simply watches, another backs away. Each reacts differently to different stimuli—fearing sounds, eagerly engaging another's eyes, ready to mouth anything. There is no right or wrong, only different. So offering each material to a particular child is a surprise for the teacher—will it please, startle, amuse? The range of children's approaches and reactions allows teachers to observe the micro-seconds in which, minute by minute, hour after hour, the neuronal networks in the brain are built. Does a child reject the feeling of paint but revel in the surround of sound? Does she handle hard objects in the same way as soft ones? Does he immediately repeat a new experience? Or is it new over many introductions? Does he attend for long or short periods? What relationships has she formed, might she form with each material?

In this chapter I consider both individual and cultural imperatives in humans' relations with materials. I explain the overlap between Reggio beliefs about materials and research from the field of neuroscience on the senses and memory. And, I describe materials in a classroom scenario.

CULTURAL CONTRASTS: 10,000 YEARS AGO AND NOW

The cultural imperatives of 10,000 years ago were closer to those of the early 1800s than those of the 1800s are to our culture, only 2 centuries removed. Sometime between the start of the Industrial Revolution and the end of World War II, changes began that altered the cultures of industrializing countries in unforeseen ways. The culture of the United States in the early 21st century reflects those changes.

10,000 Years Ago

The plateau people of the lower Columbia River in Washington State—the Yakama, the Hidatsa, and the Shoshone Native Americans—had relationships with materials that had evolved for 10,000 years or more before Lewis and Clark arrived around 1810. Hard as it is to imagine life without big-box stores, once everything humans made originated in nature, acquired meaning from its origin, expanded in meaning as it was fashioned, and deepened in meaning as it was used. Consider their use for shells: wapato for scooping, olivello for trading, abalone for beauty, dentalia as a symbol of wealth. Consider rocks and minerals: obsidian for arrowheads, basalt for mortars and pestles, jadeite for carvings and aesthetic objects. Consider deer and sheep: antlers for blowing, horns for handles, fur for clothing, hides for housing, bones for implements, sinew for binding, meat for sustenance, fat for warming. Consider corn: stalks for poles, husks for pouches, floss for weaving, cobs for dolls or pipes, seeds for food.

The "vocabulary" of seeds was vast—hundreds of seeds, not just wild rye (food) and acorns (decor, carving, trading), but whitebark pine, yellow pond lily (called "wokas"), bitterroot, cous, camas. Searching them out was a woman's full-time occupation, along with preparing, preserving, and storing them as well as other edible plants. A single family of four annually required as much as 1,500 pounds of dried roots for sustenance, to be ground with mortar and pestle and stored just so. To gather this food a woman required a digging stick and pouch. The stick had to be fashioned from a tree, rigid and strong so it would not bend or break. A rock with a cup-like shape had to be found, hollowed, and chipped so its tip was pointed and edges sharpened; then it had to be tightly bound to the stick. A food-collection pouch had to be fashioned from cork husks so it was sturdy and aesthetic; a good pouch, with colorful decorations made from dyed plant material, lasted for generations and was a girl's prized wedding gift (Sacajawea Interpretive Center, 2009).

Today

Mechanized tools powered by nonhuman energy have divorced us from materials' sources and making, obliterating our relationships with the gathering, processing, and use of materials that feed, house, or amuse us. Yet, only 2 centuries ago, if you were not a member of the small wealthy class, you used man or animal power to plant and harvest what you ate and hand-fashioned everything you used and wore. For millennia family members built shelters, crafted tools, shaped dugouts, and provided food and protection. Today's children are not raised in the midst of family production where, from infancy, they would observe the labor to gather, prepare, and store food; the effort to make warmth; and the exertion to carry water. In Colonial America 3-year-olds carried pailfuls from dawn to dusk, servants to their family's need for water. Today materials are divorced from brain and hand, and life is divorced from hand-fashioned materials. Our infants are raised not in the company of people whose purpose is to ensure survival and transmit culture but in the electronic shadows of cartoons whose purpose is to fixate children's attention and sell them products. Commercialism has invaded schools where infant/toddler furnishings alone are a $10 billion annual market.

Reggio: A Contrast. In contrast to current U.S. early education, Reggio infant/toddler centers and preschools echo traditions as old as our species—using predominantly natural materials and colors, and enabling children to use tools so they acquire facility in what Reggio educators call "100 languages." These "languages" are materials, broadly defined, each with particular characteristics and inherent properties that permit certain uses and constrain others. Collectively, the 100 languages become the very competencies Important Commissions say are required in order to be competitive in the 21st century—imagination, creativity, self-motivation, focus, and collaborative ability. While most U.S. schools need to be reconceived to foster these competencies, children in Reggio schools excel at them. There are many reasons why:

- the belief that from birth children are competent;
- the practice of working in small groups;
- teachers' role as researchers/collaborators;
- classroom practices in which teachers "listen" to children and are highly responsive;
- teachers' intentionality whereby they prepare an aesthetic, meaning-full environment and induce children to engage in meaning-full activity;
- the prevalence of documentation and its use as a means of reflection.

It is beyond this book's scope to describe these practices, but they are well documented elsewhere (Dolci, 2000; Domus Academy Research Center, 1998; Edwards, Gandini, & Forman, 1998; Lewin-Benham, 2006, 2008; Malaguzzi, 1995, 1991; Reggio Children, 2004; Rinaldi, 2006). The Reggio practice most relevant to the concept of "100 languages" is the use of diverse materials in provocative ways with the intent of fostering children's many competencies.

Disconnected Lives. As I watch the intense relationships of today's youth with superstars, and their food obsessions or drug dependencies, or when I talk with preschoolers whose only topics are Tom and Jerry or Spiderman, I see children desperate for ways to stimulate their brain because we—parents, schools, politicians, marketers—have not provided conditions in which the brain can find challenge or seek the nobler human goals. The culture of mall-rats—youth whose pastime is endless shopping but who never have enough—depicts futile attempts by young people to find something of meaning. At root I see a failure to build the brain/hand nexus that for millennia, since the start of our species, has driven us to create material cultures—and I include the arts and sciences in "material." These cultures reflect the heights of human imagination and ingenuity.

Every culture has been created, not by an individual, but by a group. That group forms a social system in which care and education of the young is the paramount means—nay the *only* means—of guaranteeing that the culture, and especially its relationships with the materials necessary for its survival, is passed on. We have today a huge disconnect between our culture and the social systems that evolved as our culture itself evolved. We also have mass abandonment of the age-old interdependent relationships between humans and materials. These factors have created social conditions that are adverse to children's well-being. The forces shaping these conditions occur on far too large a scale to prove correlation, much less causation, of the reasons why children are bored, pressured, or angry, why they are overmedicated, why they seek harmful stimulation, and why many of their behaviors are obsessive. Recently, increasingly young children, now as young as 4 years old, have become pawns in the attempt to make teachers accountable for children's successful and timely performance of the particular group of brain functions we call reading. In many schools the time devoted to literacy has eclipsed the meager time for using materials, time that was a remnant of a former, gentler era. Sadly, what we call literacy—mastering decoding skills—is merely a sliver of what a truly literate culture imbues in its children.

In my opinion, remedies lie in reconnecting children's relationships with materials and with others. Harry Chugani (2004) says, "It is now evident that children exposed to early social deprivation suffer long-term cognitive and behavioral deficits associated with dysfunction in brain regions known to be damaged by prolonged stress" (p. 8). Scenarios in this book show children's engagement with other humans and with materials from infancy. Relationships among other, material, and brain not only form the individual; they also form a culture of learning that is essential to sustain the collective brain of a society.

> It is essential to remember that every time we invest attention in an idea, a written word, a spectacle; every time we purchase a product; every time we act on a belief; the texture of the future is changed, even if in microscopic ways. The world in which our children and their children will live is built, minute by minute, through the choices we endorse with our psychic energy. It is not only the legislation we help pass, the wars we help wage, the great inventions and works of art that will shape the future, but also our small habits of mind and behavior: the way we talk to our children, how we spend our free time, whether we always increase the consumption of finite resources or whether we find ways to live within less wasteful limits. These small choices, these trivial decisions, have as much weight in the long run as all of Napoleon's wars. (Csikszentmihalyi, 1993, pp. 167–168)

REGGIO AND NEUROSCIENCE RESONANCES

The use of materials in Reggio schools is based on a theory of human development, a science of materials' properties, and the discipline of design. Each expressive language reflects a particular structure: Because they combine the rational, imaginative, cognitive, and sensitive aspects of the brain, expressive languages are "the most effective antibodies to violence and the most conducive means for listening to others and the world" (Domus, 1998, p. 15). Here we see how Reggio beliefs about materials resonate with neuroscience; we examine Reggio ideas about development, materials, and design; and we watch how these ideas translate into classroom experiences.

Materials, Senses, and Memory

The Italian language contains an adjective, "materico"; it means a material's varied and unique properties, in other words, its essence. Reggio educators believe that infants and toddlers are capable of perceiving a material's essence because in their first months of life they perceive the world with a kind of "sensory plasticity" (Domus, 1998, p. 16). Biological imperatives drive sensory exploration, which leads to discrimination and ultimately to meaning-making. Sensory experience is the foundation for memory. Because dull environments deaden sensory perceptions, infant/toddler environments *must* be designed to nurture and develop sensory perception so that it sharpens and becomes refined (Domus, 1998).

Synesthetic Experience. Reggio educators have adapted the word *synesthetic*, which in neuroscience means "the fusions of different senses" (Sacks, 2007, p. 179). Reggio designers try to create experiences that cause synesthesia yet, at the same time, preserve the qualities of individual materials so that they can be distinctly perceived. They do this by mixing visual/tactile, hearing/shape, or any combination of contrasting and overlapping sensory experiences (Domus, 1998).

There is some evidence that such "hyper-connectivity" is indeed present in primates and other mammals during fetal development and early infancy, but is reduced or "pruned" within a few weeks or months after birth. There have not been equivalent anatomical studies in human infants, but as Daphne Maurer of McMaster University notes, behavioral observations of infants suggest "that the newborn's senses are not well differentiated, but instead are intermingled in a synaesthetic confusion." (Sacks, 2007, p. 193)

Synesthesia and Memory. Sensory cues trigger memory. Ratey (2002) explains the astounding feats of mnemonist S. V. Shereshevski who could precisely recall amazing amounts of unrelated detail. He says Shereshevski perceived "with criss-crossed senses" (p. 203), hearing shapes, seeing tastes, feeling numbers. Hearing a tone of 2,000 cycles per second, he said, "It looks something like fireworks tinged with a pink-red hue." Or, "The strip of color feels rough and unpleasant, and it has an ugly taste—rather like a briny pickle. You could hurt your hand on this" (p. 203). Current neuroscience calls Shereshevski's "talent" synesthesia. It means that a stimulus triggers an unrelated sense. For example, seeing color when you hear music is not merely in the mind but is a sensation someone actually experiences: He hears musical notes but sees colors.

Memory and the Senses. Ratey uses synesthesia as an example of the importance of sensory experience in creating memories. Sensory experiences make up a great deal of our memories. Try to remember anything and notice the amount of sensory information—how things looked, sounded, felt, or smelled. PET scans and fMRI have changed the age-old question from, Where are memories stored, to, What is memory—storage space? act? retrieval strategy? search? or formation? In fact, memory is all of these (Ratey, 2002).

Memories don't sit in the brain waiting for us to recall them. Memory is an active process. Memories can be seen only in brain scans as a person is in the process of remembering because when we remember we retrieve bits from different networks in the brain. What we remember includes our feeling, the place, and the emotional tenor at the time of the experience. Because experiences are personal, different people remember the same event differently. Moreover, as people change over time, they recall the same event differently. As our attitude changes, so does what and how we remember (Ratey, 2002).

How Memory Works. Cellular biophysicist Eric Kandel received the Nobel Prize in Medicine in 2000 for explaining how the brain stores long-term memories. He identified the molecular changes that occur in the brain when an animal learns something.

> Spaced repetition [of the stimulus] convert[s] the memory for short-term habituation and sensitization to longer-lasting memories. . . . Even though the anatomical connections between neurons develop according to a definite plan, the strength and effectiveness of those connections is not fully determined developmentally and can be altered by experience. . . . The capability for behavioral modification seems to be built directly into the neural architecture of the behavioral reflex. (Kandel, 2001)

One type of memory, called episodic, means remembering actual experiences. It involves many parts of the brain—perception in the posterior cortex, capture and initial storage in the prefrontal cortex, holding for a short while in the frontal lobes' working memory, retrieval after this short while by the hippocampus and placement back in the frontal lobes, which are pivotal in holding and manipulating words and spatial representations. The other type of memory, called procedural, means remembering routines, like how to get dressed, how to fry an egg, or how to hit a softball (Ratey, 2002).

Kandel (2006) states that there are

three important principles of the biological basis of memory. First, memory is a distinct mental function, clearly separate from other perceptual, motor, and cognitive abilities. Second, short-term memory and long-term memory can be stored separately. . . . Third, . . . at least one type of memory can be traced to specific places in the brain. . . . Short-term, explicit memory for people, objects, places, facts, and events is stored in the prefrontal cortex. These memories are converted to long-term memories in the hippocampus and then stored in the parts of the cortex that correspond to the senses involved. . . . Implicit memories of skills, habits, and conditioning [also called procedural] are stored in the cerebellum, striatum, and amygdala. (pp. 129–130)

Repetition impresses events in memory.

Repetition and Memory

Throughout this book I stress the importance of using materials in repetitive ways, but varying experiences to ensure that children pay attention. Our evidence that infants are engaged, not bored, is the nuances of their behavior—attraction toward, slight head turn, prolonged eye contact, body orientation, smile, focused eyes, reaching hands. These are the languages infants use before they develop the movements and brain connections required for speech.

Repetitive experiences engage different tactile/visual/proprioceptive/gustatory/olfactory/auditory receptors, each of which, alone and in combination, hones specialized neural networks. Infants self-stimulate to create an infinite number of games that keep the brain active as they simultaneously process with different senses. Materials are the "stuff" of infant games. They stimulate infants to pursue their activities and provide the variety that maintains interest. In time repetition of an activity trains different parts of the brain to work smoothly together. The brain teaches itself through repetition and variety, and lays in a store of experiences that—as the brain grows, neuronal networks increase, and language develops—form the basis for memory.

THE DESIGN AND DEVELOPMENT OF MATERIALS

Every animal selects its food, chooses an environment that supports its habits, and picks a particular mate. Humans have raised selection processes to new levels of particularity. Reggio educators set new horizons for the consideration of materials, deeply aware that what they select and its inherent design and qualities can impact children's development.

Materials' Individuality

In selecting materials, Reggio teachers consider each material's individuality and unusual features such as shape, pressure, temperature, and the movements children must make to use the material. They describe materials with vocabulary that defines materials' properties. Surfaces are

**Leftover wood turnings spark this almost
3-year-old's imaginative block play.**

Photos by Alexandra Cruickshank Photography

- "angular, carved, clotted, coarse, compact, fibrous, firm, granite, metallic" [or they are]
- "rough, hard, pointed, refractory, rigid, solid, thick, tough" (Domus, 1998, p. 74)

Alexandra understands. She teaches toddlers. She gasped one day, visiting the shop of a woodworking friend and seeing his floor strewn with the most unusual blocks—hard, rounded, turreted, spiraled, multicolored! They were wood turnings, leftovers from his carved pieces, made from a wide assortment of woods. She pleaded for some and, months later, he sanded 50 to 60 of them. She added them to the block collection and describes:

> Zen [age 3] was building cities: "These are the towers and that's the gate." There were fountains, gardens, houses, trees; Zen knew exactly which were which, although I could not tell the difference. The towers mixed with blocks were a home to protect the kitty.

Reggio designers describe:

- Absorbent is: "damp, dank, drenched, fluid, gelatinous, greasy, gummy, impregnated, liquid, moist, oily, slimy."
- Wet is: "slushy, soaked, sodden, soggy, soupy, sticky, sweaty, tacky, viscous, watery." (Domus, 1998, p. 74)

Alonzo, age 4½, understood when, after several days of work transforming a large, intricate sculptural dinosaur into a full-scale paper representation, he referred to the process as "sweaty" (Lewin-Benham, 2006, p. 126).

Reggio designers continue:

- Cold is: "chilly, congealed, cool, frosty, frozen, gelid, glacial, glazed, icy, metallic, penetrating, steely, stone-cold, watery."
- Hot is: "arid, blazing, boiling, igniferous, incandescent, red hot, scalding, scorching, searing, steamy, tepid, torrid."

From 0 to 3 infants and toddlers establish the skills that underlie planning and analyzing so that by age 4 to 5 they can make complex constructions. Here, a 4½-year-old has made a paper rendering of a three-dimensional object in a 1:1 scale.

Photo by Jennifer Azzariti

- Dry is: "abrasive, arid, bitter, coated, crumbly, crusty, dry, dried up, fragile, frizzy, fuzzy, knotty, parched, rough, rugged, scaly, shattered, sluggish, stale."
- Soft is: "cottony, creamy, delicate, ductile, flaccid, fleecy, fleshy, flexible, floppy, hairy, limp, malleable, puffy, rubbery, silky, soft, spongy, tender, vaporous, velvety, wooly." (Domus, 1998, p. 75)

Teachers at the World Bank Children's Center make lots of materials using transparent containers, sometimes empty, sometimes with found objects inside. They understand; transparent is: glisteny, see-through, shiny, absent, rigid, cold, clear, open, unseen, light, sheer, glassy.

Infants grasp, wave, fling, slide, and explore transparent plastic containers that hold all kinds of objects that glisten, clack, or rattle in response to their movements.

Photo by Elly Solomon

Materials and Creativity

Is it any wonder that children say: "The night swallowed up the sun." Or, "The oatmeal tasted pebbly." Kornei Chukovsky, prominent Russian author and writer of the classic book on children's language *From Two to Five* (1963), adds: "A bald man has a barefoot head, a mint candy makes a draft in the mouth, the husband of a grasshopper is a daddyhopper" (p. 2). Such statements, which are considered amusing, naive, or creative, are children's synesthetic way of experiencing the world: They have not yet packaged sensory experiences with the words that commonly represent them, so conflate perception and expression, confiscating the languages of the senses and intermingling them with nouns and verbs to describe experiences. As they learn what goes with what (or as teachers *correct* how they express their perceptions), the creativity of their early years is channeled into vocabulary the culture accepts and thus the right-answer mind-set of schooling conscribes their imagination. Artists and scientists live without conscribing their imagination and are skilled in using real materials. So synesthesia becomes their realm, their creativity expressed in socially accepted forms, unless they stray too far beyond the norm.

Designing with Materials

Reggio educators call their strategic of use of materials "an expressive and poetic policy [to] balance" (Domus, 1998, p. 76) different materials' natures. They question whether common materials retain any of their *genetic* properties, or whether these have been lost in the translation to object. For some decades, from the 1800s to the 1950s as synthetic materials were produced at a rapidly increasing pace, societies prized the transformation. But in the postindustrial era we have begun to yearn for a purity in materials that reveals their "genetic" heritage (Domus, 1998, p. 76).

Today's material scenario is complex:

- different families—wood, leather, textiles, glass;
- varied durability—paper walls, ceramics, stone, plants;
- a range of grains—wide, closely striated, straight, wavy.

Homes fully reflect this complexity, but schools continue to use materials with a narrow range of properties. When Reggio educators design, they are conscious the materials will influence "diverse sensory perceptions (light, color, acoustic and microclimatic conditions, tactile effects) . . . [and] different sensory values so that each individual can tune into his or her own personal [ways of] reception" (Domus, 1998, p. 15).

Development

Infants and toddlers use the tactility of their mouths, hands, and entire bodies to explore. Their skin is like "an extremely sensitive and intelligent 'radar' . . . that senses materials' light and temperature and establishes relationships of sympathy, antipathy, and difference" (Domus, 1998, p. 76). They finger, nuzzle, pat, or stroke. Boys', girls', infants', toddlers', and preschoolers' individuality determines the different ways they use their hands:

- alone or together
- tips of fingers, palms, backs, sides, nails, knuckles

and the strategies they use as their hands and bodies explore:

- caressing lightly
- stroking repeatedly
- moving in circles
- embracing
- squeezing
- weighing

Some "listen" to what they touch, attentive, seemingly using the tactile sense to search for relationships. Others' hands seem more "opaque," less exploratory, more cursory (Domus, 1998, pp. 76–77). The implication is: If we want to foster the imagination of infants and toddlers so that it fully develops, sterile environments must become "rich and varied" with a "harmonious complexity" (p. 77).

ONE HUGE AND MANY SMALL EVENTS

Here we see two kinds of experiences with materials. One, in a Reggio infant/toddler center, consists of a single teacher-made object, a one-time Big experience. The other, at the WBCC, consists of small-scale, teacher-made objects used daily in infant classrooms.

The Colossus

In 1992 at the Reggio Infant/Toddler Center Il Girotondo, I was drawn to a documentation panel titled "La Collosa." It portrayed the infants and toddlers arriving one morning to confront in their piazza a column of cardboard, 6 feet or so in height and girth, gigantic to toddlers standing barely 2 feet high or still in a prone position. In 24 photographs, the teachers captured a series of forays in which the toddlers gradually laid the column low, finally reducing it to a huge length of rolled-out cardboard. Based on the documentation, I imagined the following scene.

Discovery. Some children crawled—bold, impatient, imperious—to investigate this giant invading their space. Using every means, they grasped a structure whose smooth curvilinear surface gave no purchase. They bumped the unyielding monolith with feet, pushed with shoulders, pummeled with fists. Others hung back—timorous, uncertain—to see what would happen, aware that distance represented immunity from this newly dominating Presence that had erased the comfortable familiarity of their space. A third group, midway between intrepid and wary, held back long enough to determine the nature of this invader, assessing whether it had the capacity to move and thereby possessed life and its defining unpredictability. Or, was it inanimate? "Infants divide the world into the animate and the inert early in life. Three month olds are upset by a face that suddenly goes inert but not by an object that suddenly stops moving" (Pinker, 1997, p. 322). They recognize that the living can strike, frighten with barks, or surprise in other threatening ways. They know nonliving entities cannot move by themselves and thus cannot maul or engulf. Ascertaining that the Presence was not alive, a number of children joined the first group, probing, poking, and punching, while the wariest remained apart.

Attack. For a full morning the infants and toddlers worked at the Presence. Perhaps with sudden insight or perhaps merely by accident, an almost 3 year old brought a marker, others copied, and a rash of scribbling ensued, changing the Presence's appearance, but not penetrating its surface. Another older toddler brought a paintbrush and, grasping the bristle end as prehistoric hunter might have grasped spear, jabbed the surface, secure that it would not jab back. Emboldened by the broad-faced attack, a bevy of toddlers brought weapons. Markers, paintbrushes, and glue sticks became vehicles that finally pierced the skin of the Presence. Those not yet standing worked flat on their bellies, joining the fray, fist clutching an implement. Those at a distance crept closer, less timorous now that the Presence was pierced with no harm to anyone.

Conquest. Suddenly, bodies pressing the newly vulnerable Presence caused an unexpected result: It tipped! The movement made many back off, again wary: Was the Presence alive? Could it retaliate? "Between eighteen and twenty-four-months, children begin to separate the contents of other people's minds from their own beliefs" (Pinker, 1997, p. 330). They knew that, were it alive, the piercing would evoke its anger. But the brave pressed forward and, mustering collective strength, pushed again. Again the Presence tipped. No one needed to remove infants from behind. All knew enough about the physics of movement and had the spatial judgment to understand that fall has directionality, that bulk occupies circumscribed space. So, infants and toddlers, with intuitive but workable knowledge of movement, distance, and force—the kind of creative knowing that formal arithmetic and elementary science lessons rarely tap—instinctively positioned themselves away from where the Presence, were it to fall, would land.

The game took on a rhythmic quality: lean . . . push . . . tip . . . back off, again and again. Then puffs and grunts began, accompanying the movement, relieving the strain, like the Volga boatmen's chant: "Yo-oh, heave, ho—o." Lee-ean–push–tip, pause. The work song, common to many cultures, sets a rhythm to heavy labor. Leaders chant an opening line and the chorus of workers answer, falling into a regular pattern to match the job. The pace intensified, the group now divided into doers and watchers, each playing its role—the doers overwhelming the Presence, the watchers an appreciative audience: Lee-ean! Push! Tip! And then, the column gave. (If you have bent a teaspoon, you know that moment: You grasp bowl in one hand, handle in the other, rhythmically pressing up and down, the forged metal at first unyielding. Then, at an indeterminate instant, it gives, seemingly melts, and the spoon bends.)

New Discovery. The column, no longer such a presence, had a new relationship to the infants and toddlers, similar to other cardboard tubes, now a more recognizable entity. We can imagine the next explorations—crawling and creeping through; playing peek-a-boo from opposite sides; nosy fingers and clutching hands working now-accessible edges; fingernails scratching seams. Ah! Those vulnerable seams became the column's undoing, although the day ended before the children's fascination waned.

The next day a few, remembering the seams, made an all-out investigation, tearing here, scraping there, scratching, pulling, rubbing, discovering that under these assaults the formerly impervious material gradually gave way. Tearing off small bits and unpeeling longer sections required the balance to stand, grasp, and pull simultaneously. Once they discovered the cardboard would rip into longer sheets, *that* became the game. Eventually, the cardboard yielded, and, wondrously, unrolled into a huge expanse—a sea of thick grey cardboard covering a substantial portion of the floor of the piazza.

And . . . The next day, assuredly, a new use would be invented and new experiences ensue, whether suggested by the teachers' intentional selection and careful placement of materials or initiated by the children's own search and with instruments of their choosing. Either way they would configure, reconfigure, and continue their alterations of La Collosa.

Teacher-Made Objects

Teachers at the WBCC have made many objects from ordinary materials, some of which are described below. All provide repetitive, varied, transformative, and novel opportunities for infants. They challenge the movement centers in the brain and strengthen connections between eye/hand, shoulder/arm/hand, neck/head, head/torso, legs/feet. They help infants build the capacity to wield implements, maintain balance, become more articulate in using their limbs, and make increasingly complex movements. They stimulate wonder and imagination. All are tributes to teachers' creativity, ingenuity, and ability to see the potential in common objects. All offer opportunities for infants to:

- interact with objects in diverse ways;
- create an infinite number of games driven by the maturational imperative to move;

- explore sensorially, sometimes one sense dominating, sometimes others used synesthetically.

All experiences hone the emerging capacity of the brain to:

- understand where the body ends and an object begins;
- distinguish between self and other;
- recognize the indivisibility of a single object;
- notice sameness or difference;
- gain a sense of agency, that is, one's own power to act so that something else reacts.

This knowledge can be gained only through the combined actions of eye and hand, hand and mouth, ear and arm, and the myriad other neuronal networks the brain is building. The more combinations the environment stimulates, the more synapses can connect in the brain, and the more relationships the brain can make. Some of the varied materials made by teachers at the World Bank Children's Center in Washington, DC, are described below.

Shake Bottles and Containers. Clear plastic containers of varied sizes sound or look different when shaken, tilted, upended, waved, or dropped because they contain different objects—glittery beads; bits of wood; natural objects, like pebbles; bottle caps, buttons, bells—one type of object per bottle, with the closures *securely glued*. Objects are lightweight so infants can handle and move the bottles easily and they produce pleasant, soft sounds. Some containers are the size sample bath products come in, others are as large as quart soda bottles or containers for a dozen apples (see the last photo in Chapter 3).

The different sizes require grasping in different configurations, fingers closed tightly or spread widely, one- or two-handed. Rattling, tipping, or dropping sound and look different, sometimes distinctly so, other times subtly. So, when an infant just slightly varies her movement, the container alerts, arrests, or renews her attention. Some qualities of sound or arrangement—specific to each container—cause long, engaged responses, different for each infant.

Finding and making objects that infants love to use engages teachers' originality and creativity.

Photos by Elly Solomon

Transparent Pouches. Clear plastic 8½ x 11" sheet protectors are each filled with a different flattish material—glitter, sequins, the smooth wooden shapes sold by craft suppliers, coarse salt dyed with food color. The quantity is enough to intrigue the infants, but fills only 15 to 20% of the space so materials will move easily on their own. This allows infants to push them around through the plastic. The edges are reinforced with wide, transparent packing tape. If tape begins to curl or accumulates grime under the edges, the pouches are thrown out and new ones made. The sheet protectors and materials cost very little and can be produced quickly.

Pouches weigh almost nothing so are easy for infants to hold. They stimulate entirely different finger and hand movements than the bottles. The hand/arm/shoulder movements of waving, sliding, or flinging cause different movement pathways in the brain to develop. Although some materials are the same as in the containers, they move and sound different in the pouches. As with the containers, infants' visual, auditory, and other senses combine in different ways when they handle the pouches.

Laminated Collections. These use objects similar to those in the pouches, but are completely flat. The teachers press whole leaves, crush leaves, and flatten flower petals and other natural objects. They cut paper shapes from a wide variety of colors, textures, and designs. They assemble some in contrasting colors, others in close hues (see discussion of color mixing in Chapter 5). Some are glisteny. Others have different degrees of opacity or transparency. As soon as infants can pull themselves up, teachers put the laminated collections on the light table. Because they are slick, infants can move them around easily. Standing over them with light glowing through, the infants gain a new perspective on the materials. Later toddlers choose pouches themselves to put on the bed of the overhead projector.

Cut Shapes. These are 5-inch forms, differently colored or patterned, and are made from lightweight cardboard. They are painted, covered with contact paper or with differently textured materials in distinct geometric shapes—circles, triangles, hexagons, rectangles. They are used alone or, as infants become more mobile and creep toward things, are hidden under paper or in cardboard tubes, stimulating infants to lift, peer into, overturn, reach for, hold, fling, or wave.

Transparent Containers. Big-box grocers package fruits, such as apples, in clear plastic containers with a large lip, perfect for grasping. It is a satisfying item for an infant because it is very large yet light enough to wave around. We can imagine the sense of power infants feel in making these objects move so freely. The empty packages fascinate and when infants' attention wanes, teachers add the kinds of lightweight objects described above. Transparent egg cartons provide similar possibilities for mouthing, moving, and shaking.

This 20-month-old explores pouches with glisteny objects, then puts them on the light table.

Photos by Jessica Gagliardi

CONCLUSION: MEANING-FULL MATERIALS

Although few in our culture make what we use, some teachers have reclaimed a direct connection with materials by repurposing what the culture produces to create objects that are ingenious and that harness children's imagination. Parents who question the purpose can be told with assurance that using such materials strengthens the brain's attention system, sensory perceptions, movement centers, spatial understanding, ability to make connections, memory, sense of wonder, and self-competence. Together these qualities constitute creativity. They are the qualities we see in artists, scientists, and other self-actualized adults. For that is where purposeful use of stimulating materials leads—to humans who are meaning-full in their endeavors; who question, care, are engaged, are creative; who contribute to their society; and thus who advance the gene pool of the species.

5

Painting
with Tempera

When I was a child, I painted like Raphael. I've spent all my life trying to paint like a child.

—Pablo Picasso

The first time I introduced paint I was so scared. We stripped the babies down to their diapers. The four youngest were 5 months old, the three others were 7 to 9 months. They used their feet, their hands, their whole bodies to explore small bits of paint I poured on about a nine-foot length of butcher paper [on the floor]. It became clear at once that it is better to work with one or two, not three or four children because you are better able to see what fascinates them. One teacher is in the experience and, at the same time, a close observer. Someone else has to take the photo. Ada hardly sat so I supported her since she found it hard even to push herself up from her tummy.

I mix my own colors because they are softer to my eye. What I choose reflects the season, a clean pleasing color. I pour a little into a baby food-sized jar and show it to the children. They do not yet have the coordination to put their hand into the jar, so I spill it on the canvass.

Akil puts in both hands, approaching the paint as if he is mastering it; he slides his foot and wipes his hands on his body. He is fearless and knows no boundaries. Other children look, see, and touch, but not with Akil's abandon. Each child stays 5 minutes or so. You know when they are finished, and some move away. The whole experience for the seven infants takes about 45 minutes and every child needs a bath after. All the teachers have to be in the mood. We try to paint once a month. The children tend to stay longer when they are more used to it.

With toddlers of 18 months and more, we go back to a finished painting and add things—found materials like ribbons, bits of wrapping papers with flowers that I cut out, a nice rose-colored paper that I cut into shapes, artificial green leaves, or items that parents donated or I found. (Elly Solomon, studio teacher, World Bank Children's Center)

In this chapter I show a teacher learning to use tempera and explain the approach she eventually adopted. I explain intentional teaching and use the Reggio schools as examples of how the relationships in an environment influence an activity like painting. I conclude with tips on beginning to paint with infants and toddlers.

STUMBLING, REFLECTING, LEARNING

Here we watch a new teacher learning how to be intentional. We see her failure, reflection, and progress.

The Experience

Danielle had a teaching degree and a year's experience teaching 7th grade when she decided to work with toddlers. Now an assistant in a toddler class, she was asked to introduce painting to four 15- to 17-month-olds.

First Trial. Danielle followed her inclination to be directive, to instruct the toddlers in how to hold a brush, remove excess paint, and stay within the confines of the paper. Within minutes she was reduced to tears. The toddlers paid no attention and spilled paint everywhere. The table was a mess, their clothes more so. Fighting back tears and embarrassed, she cleaned up. That night Danielle thought of another approach.

Second Trial. Danielle used larger sheets of painting paper on top of protective paper and a small jar with just an inch of paint for each child. She handed each child a brush. This time, the paint did not spill, but two children dabbed for a minute, then wandered off; the third upended the jar; the fourth painted her smock. Again feeling like a failure, Danielle racked her brain for an entirely different approach.

Third Trial. Danielle hung an adult-sized smock in a prominent place, visible anywhere in the classroom. At 10 o'clock, when most children were engaged, she walked purposefully to the smock. With deliberation and exaggerating each movement—working big—she reached each arm in, fastened each button, and examined the result, checking explicitly to be sure the smock completely covered her clothes. She noticed three children watching intently. Moving precisely, she protected the table, with considerable thought selected an 8½ x 14" sheet of paper, and placed it neatly in the center. Then she poured an inch of paint from a 4" tall bottle into a small jar, still exaggerating every move. She grasped the bottle in one hand, placed her other hand close to the neck to control the flow of the paint exactly, tipped the bottle so just a thin stream emerged, and turned the bottle upright instantly when the paint reached a line she had drawn on the jar. She alternately examined a collection of brushes, selectively chose one, sat at the place she had created, and proceeded to paint. Four children, the three who had been watching her and one other, left what they were doing and clustered at her table, hungrily following every move. None had taken part in her first two attempts.

With the children watching intently, she thoughtfully completed a painting of spirals, wrote her name and date, and carefully hung it to dry. She purposely folded and put away the protective paper, washed and put away the brush, poured the unused paint back into the bottle with a funnel, washed and rehung the funnel. Throughout, the children followed her. She took them to look at her painting, mindfully traced the lines with her fingers, and encouraged them to do so. She told them she had been thinking of the chambered nautilus shell when she made the painting. Did they want to see one? Their expressions said yes. All examined the shell. Danielle encouraged them to be slow and deliberate, and she engaged them in a "conversation" about the shell and the painting. As their attention waned, she settled each into an activity and with some trepidation approached the teacher. They would meet after school.

Reflection

> *Danielle*: "At first I just grabbed any children, thinking that painting was intrinsically interesting, but saw that it must not be. I decided that if *I* painted, it might lure children, might tap intrinsic interest and the tendency to imitate. But I'm unsure whether I should have made a painting. Maybe I should merely have prepared the materials then brought the children to the table."
>
> *Teacher*: "And what happened?"
>
> *Danielle*, pausing, still unsure: "Well, four children's eyes were glued to me. I guess I captured their attention."
>
> *Teacher*: "And?"
>
> *Danielle*, hesitatingly: "I guess I'll gather those four tomorrow and ask if they want to paint." The teacher remained expectant.
>
> *Danielle*: "I'm not sure. . . . Should I lay out the materials in advance or involve the children in preparing them?"
>
> *Teacher*: "What do you think they found so fascinating?"
>
> *Danielle*: "The whole process, they watched everything, really absorbed."

Progress

The next day Danielle gathered the four, simply saying, "Come, we're going to prepare to paint." She went through every step—smocks, protective paper, paint pouring, brush selection—soliloquizing as she did: "The smocks will keep our clothes *clean*." "*This* paper will keep paint off the table." "If I pour *very* slowly, I can stop at the line," and so on. Three of the four took part actively in setting up; the fourth watched intently. But all four painted, staying with the activity for 9 full minutes. Danielle commented only occasionally as they painted, selectively responsive to something pleasing about a child's effort: "Look at that bright red!" or "What huge brushstrokes you are making!"

As she led them through the process of hanging their paintings to dry and cleaning up, she resumed her explanations, a short full sentence about the meaning of each step in the process. The children especially loved washing the bristles, fascinated as Danielle held the brush under running water: "See how the paint flows out when I press the bristles between my fingers?" Then, "See how the water runs clear now?" All four rinsed bristles long after every trace of paint was gone! Even after all was cleaned up, the children's focus remained. Interested and compliant, they followed Danielle as she took them to each of their paintings in turn: "Nita, would you like to tell us about your painting?"

A THEORY OF HOW WE LEARN

Through trial, error, and critical self-reflection, Danielle stumbled onto a technique to engage toddlers in focused, sustained, intentional activity using tempera paint. Her initiative was supported by the head teacher's allowing her to experiment and being available to reflect with her afterward. It is an example of sociocultural theory in action.

Sociocultural Theory

Sociocultural theory provides a way to understand the interactions between Danielle/toddlers and Danielle/head teacher: Learning occurs when children deeply engage with teachers in "participatory, proactive, communal, [and] collaborative" ways (Bruner, 1996, p. 84). According to Vygotsky, "All uniquely human, higher forms of mental activity are derived from social and cultural contexts and are shared by members of those contexts" (Berk & Winsler, 1995, p. 12). Some early childhood professionals regard

> what the young child knows and develops as personally rather than socially constructed —a tradition that flows from Piaget's [work]. . . . The Vygotskian view is unique in that thinking is not bounded by the individual brain or mind. Instead, the "mind extends beyond the skin" and is inseparably joined with other minds. (Wertsch, 1991, in Berk & Winsler, 1995, p. 12)

"According to socio-cultural theory, forms of thinking assumed to develop universally in early and middle childhood *are much more a product of specific contexts and cultural conditions than was previously believed*" (Berk & Winsler, 1995, p. 18, emphasis added).

Danielle's experience reflects these central aspects of sociocultural theory. She did not give up after her initial failures, but instead became "participatory, proactive, communal, [and] collaborative" (Bruner, 1996, p. 84). The "context" she created to engage children included:

- group activity,
- children's choice,
- intentionally modeling the specific techniques that accomplish a piece of work,
- using a logical, step-by-step process,
- teacher collaboration with children,
- precise language.

Thus, she created both a context—the procedures involved in painting—and a culture—the group activity.

The Role of Language

Danielle's use of language reflects another central aspect of Vygotsky's theory, the essential role of language in thinking. "For Vygotsky language is the 'tool of the mind' . . . , the most frequently and widely used human representational system" (Berk & Winsler, 1995, p. 21). The infant/toddler years are the ideal time to lay foundations for higher level thinking, which develops through "cultural tools" that "originate on the social level, and . . . are eventually internalized" (Vygotsky, in Berk & Winsler, 1995, p. 5). "Language, the primary cultural tool used by humans to mediate their activities, is instrumental in restructuring the mind and in forming higher-order, self-regulated thought processes" (Berk & Winsler, 1995, p. 5).

Painting and all the procedures to prepare, to clean up, and to reflect are higher order, self-regulated thought processes, as are the routines and skills required to use any material. Danielle's instinctive use of language as an integral part of the activity—short, to-the-point explanations, not lectures—encouraged both self-regulation and higher order thinking.

The Role of Self-Regulation

Self-regulation is children's ability to direct their own actions to accomplish some task. It is the metacognitive aspect of the brain's attention system, the part of the brain's executive function that watches itself in action and makes corrections. Recent research on early education teaching practices suggests that self-regulation "often must begin with fairly directive efforts to reduce . . . inappropriate behavior" (Berk & Winsler, 1995, p. 96). Yet, many teachers are not taught how to use "fairly directive efforts" to manage behavior, nor are they taught how to help children become self-regulated. There is also confusion because of the Piagetian concepts of "readiness" and "stages." The Piaget tradition encourages the belief that children will do something when they are "ready," or at the stage when the behavior or thinking will occur naturally. In practice "readiness" has been extended well beyond the cognitive realm that Piaget intended and this has led some teachers to take a laissez-faire approach: They do not intervene to show a child a technique, provide language, or collaborate on next steps. Some even ignore unfocused behavior.

In a Piaget-based classroom, teachers de-emphasize conveying knowledge verbally, through didactic instruction. . . . Because Piaget's theory stresses the supremacy of development over learning, the teacher's contribution to the process of acquiring new knowledge is reduced relative to the child's. In . . . the Piagetian approach . . . [the child] tak[es] responsibility for change in a social environment that *refrains from interfering with natural development.* (Berk & Winsler, 1995, p. 103, emphasis added)

Some children self-regulate on their own but others require modeling, highly intentional teaching, and directive intervention. In the Model Early Learning Center we used highly directive efforts, intervening often, to help children become self-regulated (Lewin-Benham, 2006, 2008). Self-regulation is an essential part of children's learning to concentrate, which comes about as they train the brain's attention system through focused activity.

Summary

Danielle, driven by feelings of failure, became an intentional modeler. As she observed more and more carefully to learn what interested each child, she changed her behavior, realizing that her modeling was a potent cognitive and social force. She also learned that her intervention—*not* natural development, stages, or readiness—was the reason the children settled into an activity. She learned that how she structured and modeled an activity was the key to children's interest and self-regulation.

TEACHING WITH INTENTION

How teachers teach matters. Researchers "are developing new ways to measure how teachers interact with children," according to Klein & Knitzer (2007), who say that *intentional teaching* requires children to think in increasingly complex ways and requires teachers to be sensitive, focused, and collaborative. They advocate techniques that are "*directive* without using drill and kill strategies; . . . [are] fun for young children and promote positive peer and teacher interactions" (p. 3, emphasis added). I would add children's interest as a necessity to catch and sustain their attention.

Danielle learned from her experience to watch for signs of a child's interests, then to clearly model the activity as she succinctly narrated the procedures. A child's interests depend on his/her innate disposition, prior experiences, and the materials in the environment. What brings joy is personal, but group influence is a powerful force in spurring interest. Above all Danielle learned that preparing the environment, then listening and observing, are essential to stimulate interest, and that modeling and narration are essential to whether or how some children take to a particular activity.

Listening/Observing

Listening is a teaching skill that means using not just ears but eyes and emotions to discern children's interests, awareness, and receptivity. It means reading the nuances of children's body language. Carlina Rinaldi (2006), pedagogical director of the Reggio Schools, refers to listening as the basis for children's "creation and consolidation of concepts" (p. 67). Listening is the ultimate reciprocal activity, a two-way exchange, whether or not a word is spoken. Frances Hawkins, the brilliant preschool teacher, spent a year with profoundly deaf children, as described in her classic book *The Logic of Action* (1986). She explains why children listen to her: "I expect them to listen, [and] ask appropriate questions. It . . . requires . . . courtesy . . . and genuine intellectual curiosity about the dynamics of young children. . . . The ear and mind become tuned because the adult is not giving half-baked attention" (personal communication, May 8, 1985).

In her first two attempts Danielle did not listen; in her third she modeled, using precise movements and every nuance of human expression to send her message. In her fourth attempt she was exquisitely attuned to the children's reception and response. These are the characteristics of the kind of listening/observation that marks intentional teaching and is the bedrock of teacher/child interactions in Reggio schools.

Mediation

Reuven Feuerstein says that learning occurs through mediation. By this he means that teachers must intervene with the intention (1) to alert children's attention system; (2) to select a particular meaning in the stimulus and convey it; and (3) to go beyond the immediate experience by encouraging children to connect it to memories of prior experiences or imaginings of future ones (Feuerstein et al., 2006). Feuerstein's profound theories extend the implications in Vygotsky's slim beginnings. Vygotsky and Feuerstein, motivated by different circumstances, both arrived at an explanation of human development that differs markedly from Piaget's idea of naturally unfolding stages as the determinant of a child's capacity for certain kinds of thinking at specific ages. While teachers definitely should know about stages in growth, they also should know that, because developmental timing varies immensely from child to child, "waiting" for a stage or teaching to stage-determined benchmarks lowers the bar for what children can accomplish.

Among Feuerstein's many contributions to sociocultural theory are his theory of the Mediated Learning Experience and its robust practical applications. Danielle's fourth attempt at painting was the essence of mediation: She had an intention in mind, which she communicated powerfully. She conveyed specific meaning at each step in the process by using language to orchestrate, elucidate, and provide content (not lecture). She extended children's thinking—*transcend* is Feuerstein's word—first by showing them how her painting reflected something in her mind, then by asking them to connect their paintings to their thoughts through the medium of language.

A CULTURE OF RELATIONSHIPS

Reggio infant/toddler centers engage children from as young as 6 to 8 months in using tempera paint. The activity is embedded in a context in which the formation of relationships is a central, driving principle. Relationships pervade

- the design of the schools;
- the selection of specific materials from a varied array;
- how materials are displayed;
- interactions among children, space, and materials;
- participation of children in one another's activities;
- frequent, thoughtful, and deep intervention by teachers.

These factors shape the school experience.

School Design

Many influences shape an environment's quality:

- the shape of spaces,
- the relation between a space's function and how it is organized,
- the richness and diversity of the stimuli,
- the visual accessibility of activities from different areas of the school.

In Reggio schools glass walls and doors or many windows provide access from almost anywhere in the school to a piazza, from most classrooms to the outdoors, and from one room to another.

Piazza. The piazza contains equipment and materials to be used by any child in the school. Examples are: a kaleidoscope, mirrored inside, large enough for a group of children to crawl into; original climbing structures, not only typical steps, rockers, and balance boards; "disguise closets" to keep dress-up clothes organized; and a structure that can be changed to become now a ship, now a castle, now a mountain. A piazza could contain a piece of soft sculpture, such as several abutting large, thick floor mats made from sturdy foam that cave under your weight in some places and remain firm in others, in harmonizing colors, and coverings that are easy to clean. Because children can lift and fit these foam pieces together in various ways, their surfaces undulate unpredictably, causing surprise and challenging the body to be more coordinated (Fontanili, 2007). The piazza could contain a tennis ball, life-size scale, cut on the line where its halves intersect, and of a weight children can move easily. They rock in the ball's halves, "hide in them, or have tête-à-têtes, deconstruct or reconstruct the 'ball'" (Fontanili, 2007, pp. 88–89).

Atrium. Through glass walls children see intriguing plants and animals outdoors, natural objects that vary in movement potential, color, shape, and texture. Among them hangs children's art. The scene is reflected in mirrors that are embedded in tiles on the ground or that cover small tables.

Atelier. Literally an artist's studio, the *atelier* is a repository for a great wealth of materials and is home base for an *atelierista* (artist/studio teacher) who is both proficient in exploiting the potential in materials and interested in learning what kinds of relationships children can form with materials and with one another through their use of materials. From their earliest months, children watch one another actively investigating the *atelier's* varied materials.

These unusual spaces form a changing tapestry of children exploring materials in diverse ways. The aesthetic tableaux and soft color palette establish an awareness of movement and a visual sensitivity. Eventually the spaces inform how children wield a paintbrush and color paper with paint. We are, after all, what we see as much as what we eat.

Particular Materials

Three important aspects of materials are selection criteria, display, and variety. Each impacts the experiences infants and toddlers can have with the materials.

Selection Criteria. Reggio teachers select materials for specific activities according to many criteria:

- What is the purpose of the activity?
- What materials will fulfill the purpose?
- Among different possible choices, which are aesthetic?
- Is the material suitable for the experience?
- Does the material really work?
- Will a material last? Or will it disintegrate?
- Is a material's size and weight such that infants and toddlers can handle it?
- How many variations are possible with a given material?
- What are the material's aesthetic qualities?

With brushes, for example, bristles can be natural or synthetic, hold more or less paint, be pliable to different degrees, and leave strokes of paint that are more or less solid, and vary from narrow to wide.

Display. A huge variety of materials is displayed in transparent containers on open shelves so that items are visually accessible. Glass jars, full of materials, are displayed in orderly and aesthetic ways—short to tall, short–tall–short, or some other harmonic. Colors are graded—dark to light; subtle to bold, or in a limited spectrum, like red–orange–yellow. Size, shape, color, and texture are intentionally juxtaposed to complement or contrast with one another. In these ways displays draw children's attention. Once attending, children can make selections because materials are readily accessible. The constraints of a material—which children recall from past use—challenge children to select thoughtfully. Experiences with materials are inseparable from thinking.

In the *atelier* designed by Elly Solomon and Patrick Manning, studio teachers at the World Bank Children's Center, shelving units are modular and nestle in L-shaped arrangements. One arrangement contains masses of dyed wool, subtle shades in tactilely sensuous clouds that beg you to plunge in your hands.

Another arrangement has only blacks and whites, 30 or more natural or man-made materials—white beans, black twigs, curls of black celluloid in circular white containers. Another has silver and bronzes, a gallon of "silver dollars" (the plant), acorns spray-painted silver, a dozen dishes made from concave brown shells with bronzed seeds of many varieties, one kind per shell. The range of colors, the beauty of the containers, the juxtaposition of textures beg you to touch. Here and there the *atelierista* has placed a small metal sculpture of an animal, a tall boulder (shaped and painted to resemble a gowned woman), or other one-of-a-kind items. Wherever you look there is something awe-inspiring. Ensuring that displays are aesthetic is the *atelierista*'s responsibility.

Variety. Variety is important in maintaining or renewing interest. If the brush I used yesterday left traces of bristle marks but today's leaves solid streaks, today's experience is new. Variety requires 2- and 3-year-olds to exercise their innate capacity for visual sensitivity and cognizance of nuance.

Chukovsky (1963) comments on nuance in children's learning to speak.

The minutest variation in grammatical form is apprehended by the child, and, when he needs to contrive (or recreate in his memory) one word or another, he applies precisely that suffix or . . . grammatical word ending which . . . is essential for the needed nuance or meaning or image . . . [introducing] critical evaluation, analysis, and control . . . with a special, heightened sensitivity to the materials of speech . . . , a process he accomplishes unconsciously in his two-year-old mind. (pp. 7–10)

Chukovsky (1963) noted at least 70 grammatical forms children had mastered by the end of year 3: "Most of these 'generalizations' that are formed in the child's brain forever, for his entire life, are established between the ages of three and four, when the linguistic giftedness seems to be particularly strong" (p. 11). Pinker calls 3 year olds grammatical geniuses. Current research suggests that the process starts at 3 months or earlier. The languages of materials—each with its own minute variations—are acquired as readily in the first 3 to 4 years of life.

"100 Languages." What Reggio educators show us is the influence of an environment on everything children do, how the precociousness of the infant/toddler brain extends to a limitless array of "languages." They use the word *language* as a metaphor for children's ability to learn virtually any form of expression that is within human capacity. Thus, the effortless absorption of case, plurality, and tense extends to the "grammar" and rules of other-than-language materials. Adults naturally provide infants and toddlers with a full range of linguistic "materials." The significance of Reggio practices is the extension of infant/toddler capacities into *all* realms of human expression. Thus, we can supply all sorts of bristles, trusting that a brain prone to notice nuance in spoken language also will notice nuance in concrete materials. So, bring on the many-bristled brushes, variously textured papers, and wealth of colors that will stimulate children to speak the language of paint.

Interactions and Interventions

Loris Malaguzzi rode his bicycle to the city of Reggio Emilia, decided to stay, and ultimately, until the end of his life, was the inspiring force behind the emergence and evolution of the Reggio Approach. In the same year as that bike ride, and decades before sociocultural theory would be discovered by Americans, Chukovsky (1963) said:

> The young child acquires his linguistic and thinking habits only through communication with other human beings. It is only this association that makes a human being out of him, that is, a speaking and thinking being. But if this communication with other human beings did not evoke in him, for even a short period of time, a special heightened sensitivity to the materials of speech which adults share with him, he would remain, to the end of his days, a foreigner in the realm of his own language. (p. 9)

It is educators' responsibility to ensure that children are not "deprived of the possibility of familiarizing themselves creatively" (Chukovsky, 1963, p. 9) with the "grammar" of tempera, brushes, paper, and other materials that lend themselves to experiences involving painting. The teacher's role is to encourage infants and toddlers to form relationships with materials. Teachers who do, provide powerful ways for children to develop a disposition to *want* to engage in meaningful activity, the skill to *be able* to do so, and the *creativity* to have something to say.

BEGINNING USE OF TEMPERA

If you are not an artist or lack familiarity with tempera and other paints, use this section as a guide to brushes, paper, and tips on painting.

Brushes and Bristles

Paintbrushes that best fit 6- to 8-month-olds' hands are rounds, #5 or #7. Round bristles hold paint better than flat bristles and don't require children to flip the brush over to use all the paint they have dipped. Because long handles may tip jars over, poke children in the eye, or be awkward for first uses, I advise cutting down the handles to a length of about 7 inches and filing rough edges. Contrary to marketing, fat chunky brushes are difficult for small hands to maneuver. They absorb a lot more paint than children might want to use in their first experiences. There are many kinds of bristle heads; thinner and thicker ones are better saved for infants older than 8 months or after first painting experiences.

Paper

Medium-weight paper (lighter than construction paper but heavier than newsprint) takes paint well. For beginning experiences, color shows up best on white paper, which offers the most dramatic contrasts, makes color look more vibrant, and does not compete with paint colors; thus, children can see their strokes more clearly. Good size paper for table-top painting is 8½ x 11" or larger; the paper doesn't need to be huge because toddlers who are not yet standing or walking will not be able to reach the part farthest from them.

Jars

Clear, wide-mouthed, low containers like squat jelly jars or baby food jars work well because children can see the color through the container. Glass baby food jars reveal color better than semitransparent commercially available plastic jars. If you use the latter, remove the brush wiper; they add an unnecessary complication for toddlers in taking the brush in and out. Jars that are too high tip when children put brushes in and take them out. Fill jars about one-third full, enough almost to cover the bristles of the brush, but not the ferrule (metal part of the brush). If the paint is too high, it covers the handle, messes hands, makes brushes slippery, and smudges paintings.

Paint and Color

Tempera paint is a satisfying medium. Be sure to use a good quality (se Appendix B). Have on hand red, yellow, blue, white, and black. Colors straight out of the jar are bright and garish. Add a little white or black or a dash of a complementary color to tone colors down and give them some depth. Mix other colors to achieve a range like that on a color mixing chart. For information on color mixing, see http:// www.sugarcraft.com/catalog/coloring/colormixingchart.htm. Save metallics, fluorescents, glitter, and other special paints until infants are more experienced.

When beginning to use multiple colors, it helps aesthetically to use colors that mix without making *mud*. Try colors in the same family, like reds, yellows, and oranges, or two primary colors, for example, reds and blues. Avoid complementary color pairs like yellow/purple, red/green, and blue/orange, and combinations that contain all three primary colors (red, blue, yellow) or all three secondary colors (orange, green, purple). These turn brown when blended.

Smocks

I recommend using smocks (see Appendix B). Environments, Inc., sells one with Velcro at the waist and neck. Or use an old shirt, but make sure it is not too big. Elastic, Velcro, and some cutting and sewing can turn old shirts into effective smocks.

Easels

As soon as toddlers can hold something in their hand while standing comfortably, they can use an easel. Purchase a simple A-frame adjustable easel with a movable tray. Drilling extra holes enables you to move the board and tray down

Paint is a satisfying medium because there is no right or wrong way to use it. Toddlers gradually learn techniques that enable them to carry out their intentions more precisely.

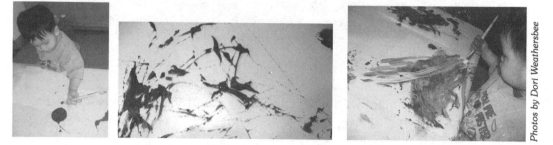

Photos by Dori Weathersbee

for a very young child. Put the paper at the center of his reach. At the MELC we built oversized A-frame easels that eliminated long spindly legs and brought the painting surface within about 4 inches of the floor.

Have on hand a damp cloth to wipe spills, drips, hands, or brush handles. Newspaper, an old sheet, plastic yard goods, or shower curtains cover a table effectively. *Caution*: If you use these coverings on the floor, tape edges securely so no one trips.

Beginning Table-Top Painting

Children's first strokes are often broad. They have a tendency to paint in the same spot on the page, which is fine. Begin with only one color. Place paint to the right or left of the child, depending on hand preference, if known. When you add a second color, make sure it is in the same color family or is a color that will mix well and not turn *muddy* (see discussion of color mixing above). When painting with more than one color, put one brush in each jar so there is no need to rinse brushes in water between colors. Rinsing is tedious, messy, and beyond toddlers' capacity. It is helpful to have a damp cloth nearby for messy hands, drips, or spills.

After a child has painted a number of times, try encouraging her to paint on the blank parts of the paper, not over and over in the same spot. Without intervention children usually will not stop painting when the paper is fully covered.

By about 20 months, children can play a game to try to cover all the white on the page with color. When the paper begins to get full, ask the child if he would like to have another piece of paper or do another painting.

Painting at an easel involves a different technique. With the child at your side, show her the paper. Run your hand over it and explain: "This is where you will put the paint." Have her feel the entire sheet with her hands. Use one color at a time with one brush. After many explorations introduce the idea of wiping the brush. Some children try to "pick up" a drip with the brush or to paint over the drip because it is not what they intended. This is an ideal time to explain that if she doesn't want the paint to drip, she can wipe the brush. Demonstrate how to hold the jar with one hand and remove the extra paint from the bristles by wiping them on the edge of the jar.

This 25-month-old figures out a technique to stop drips on his own.

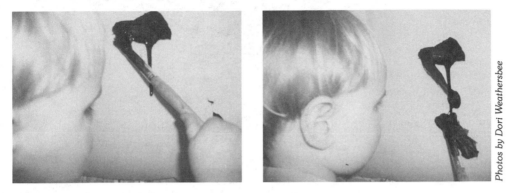

Photos by Dori Weathersbee

Scenario

When William was 15 months old, Jennifer invited him to sit at the table and paint, his first experience with tempera. He immediately dipped the brush in the jar and drew its bristles over the paper. Jennifer was unsure whether he knew this instinctively or from watching his older brother. Infants in a center where older children paint will have watched the process.

Jennifer explains:

William had used watercolors before and drawn with markers and crayons often. From these experiences, he learned that paper has a boundary and to work within it. I didn't have to say anything—he picked up the brush and started painting. He liked to touch the bristles when the brush

The first time he uses paint and brush William knows what to do and enjoys both the feeling of the paint and the act of painting.

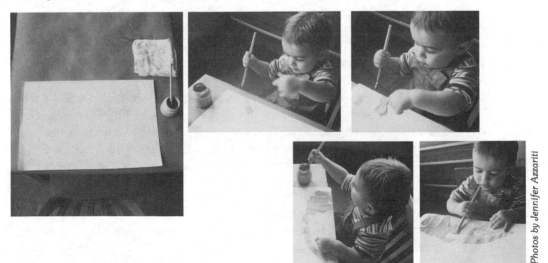

Photos by Jennifer Azzariti

Because the infant is too young to sit on her own, Elly holds her so she can reach the paint.

Photo by Krystal Walker

was full and to feel the marks immediately after making them. I had to encourage him to get more paint when his brush dried out. He was very forceful with the brush, really pushing down hard on it. Holding his hand lightly I said, "Like this, gently, as if you're petting Bunny" (our cat). He painted for about 5 minutes and then lost interest. He was teething today. (Jennifer Azzariti, personal interview, February 2009)

Jennifer lets children paint as long as they like.

It is natural for children to want to explore the paint with their hands. Marilyn Weinman, who taught high school art for 30 years, responded to her grandchild's painting his hands by giving him paper to make hand prints. At the World Bank Children's Center, teachers know infants will be covered in paint, so strip them to their diaper and give them a bath afterward. Every adult has a different tolerance for mess. If an infant's painting exceeds yours, gently redirect him. You can say something like: "Paint goes on the paper." Then, wipe his hands and continue.

CONCLUSION: THE JOY OF PAINTING

Painting provides a bang for the buck: Colors are vibrant, some bristles leave wide traces, and exciting effects emerge even in initial experiences. Infants and toddlers who are drawn to painting learn they have the power to make something dramatic happen and thereby develop what psychologists call a "sense of agency." Painting requires focus and self-control and exemplifies engaged learning. These are the basis for self-confidence. They are the mark of a lifelong attitude that disposes a person to tackle and accomplish significant work, work that is creative, original, complex, and competent. "Work is significant when it provokes young children to draw deeply on the vast store of innate capacities that are particular to humans" (Lewin-Benham, 2008, p. 3).

6

Clay

The most powerful tactic . . . to awaken the curiosity of a child . . . is simply to head for the hands.

—Frank Wilson (1998)

New at sitting, 6-month-old Mattie was fastened in a baby seat so she would not slide off. The teacher sat close by. In front of Mattie was a big block of artist's clay, the first she had ever seen. Intensely, she leaned toward it but made no attempt to touch it. Pointedly, the teacher broke some clay off the block. It was a sizable hunk with a lump protruding from the top. Mattie's eyes widened but her hands made no move. Gently the teacher took one of Mattie's hands in her own, and placed it on the lump. Mattie closed her fingers around the lump and as she did, lifted her other hand and laid it on the block. Calmly, the teacher repositioned Mattie's hand from the block so both the baby's hands were on the hunk, one on the lump at top, the other near the bottom. Slowly, the teacher put her own hands on the opposite side of the hunk and tilted it. Mattie, arms fully extended, both hands on the clay, held on as the hunk moved, her eyes widening with surprise! Deliberately, the teacher tilted it the other way. Rhythmically, teacher and baby began to rock the hunk this way and that in reciprocal action. Mattie's grip becoming firmer. When the teacher removed her hands, Mattie continued to "rock" the clay by herself, but shortly removed her hands and turned away. Her teacher interpreted this as her saying, "Enough."

Scenarios in this chapter show beginning works in clay. I describe how clay can encourage children to take on new challenges and to use their hands in entirely new ways, and what it means for the brain.

6-MONTH- AND 2-YEAR-OLD REACTIONS

The brains of 6-month-olds and 24-month-olds differ. But initial experiences are equally important for both, as the following scenarios show.

6-Month-Old Mattie

Two days later when the teacher sat Mattie in front of the clay, she reached immediately for the hunk and with no prompting rocked it back and forth. When she

At first 6-month-old Mattie is
hesitant to touch the clay . . .

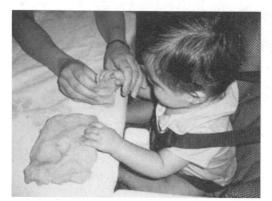

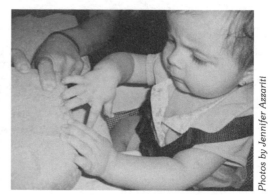

. . . but with her teacher's gentle guidance,
Mattie quickly learns to enjoy touching it.

stopped, the teacher showed her something new. Extending her finger in a precise, intentional gesture, the teacher firmly pressed down on the clay, making an impression as deep as a marble. Mattie imitated, then continued making impressions. As before, the teacher stopped when Mattie's attention waned.

The next week two hunks of clay awaited. The teacher took one and, with the same precision as before, gouged out bits. Mattie reached for the bigger hunk with her left hand, four fingers on the top, thumb pressed against the side. Then she used the thumb and index finger of her right hand to gouge bits of clay, a mixture of wonder and pleasure on her face, her mouth fixed, her eyes concentrated, as young children do when they are deeply engaged. She continued picking for 5 minutes, long for a 6-month-old. In three experiences over a week, with her teacher's intentional guidance, Mattie began to learn about artists' clay.

Artists' clay is an entirely different medium than play-dough. It is dug from the earth; play-dough is made from flour, salt, water, and coloring. Artists' clay is firm, resistant until worked, capable of being shaped with sculpting tools, and able to be stuck together with slip (glue made from clay and water). It remains as it was sculpted and can be fired in a kiln. Play-dough is usually scrunched up when a child finishes and returned to its container. If not, it dries and crumbles.

For the same reasons I prefer glue to glue sticks (see Chapter 2), I prefer artists' clay to play-dough. Artists' clay is a material used for serious purposes in diverse applications. Play-dough is a substance for children only that does not admit real applications or evoke significant accomplishment. The challenge of working artists' clay causes children to use their hands with greater strength and precision. It waits, perhaps over many days, draped in a damp cloth, for a child to continue shaping it. It can be formed in whatever ways a brain can conceive of mass—large, bulky, tiny, intricate, faceted, applied, gouged out, built up. Its surface can be smooth or textured with striations, stipples, ripples, grains, bumps, hollows, or points. Professional artists, 6-month-olds, and 24-month-olds can use it.

Photos by Jennifer Azzariti

Four 24-Month-Olds

Arthur covered the large table in the studio with butcher paper. Its slick surface protected the table from the clay's moisture; its whiteness set off the clay's deep grey color. He gathered four toddlers, 24 to 30 months old. In school just 2 months, they were about to have their first experience handling clay.

Selecting Children and Material. Arthur selected these four because, having observed their different responses to new experiences, he hoped they would influence one another. Derrick, no matter what material, plunged right in, barely seated before reaching for the material, ready to explore by himself, too eager to wait for demonstrations. Jeffrey was the opposite, watching a long time before even touching, intense, as if enacting in his brain what other children did with their hands. Georgia was distractible, often failing to become absorbed, soon drifting away to something else. But Georgia loved Maria and continually sought her company. Although they were the same age, Maria's role was protector. With Maria, Georgia was more likely to pursue an activity, although Maria, not the material, was the attraction. Maria herself was deeply attracted to some materials, barely to others. Arthur hoped clay would be to her liking.

Arthur had questions.

- How would the different dispositions of these four influence their reactions to clay?
- What might stretch their different capacities?
- Would Derrick be challenged by using the wire cutter?
- Would Jeffrey be motivated to put his hands on the clay because three other children did?

Maria might find the clay compelling since she liked soft materials such as paint and glue better than hard materials like blocks or cardboard. Georgia might explore by imitating Maria's behavior.

Arthur understood the significance of groups. As Wilson (1998) explains:

- The members are attuned to one another's unique skills.
- Each one's different skill spurs others to imitate.
- In groups, individuals demonstrate their own capacities and acquire one another's capacities through imitation.

Each group member's attention is focused on "contributions that are authentically important to the group" (p. 180).

Arthur selected clay because clay:

- can be used with hands alone,
- can be used with tools,
- appeals strongly to the tactile sense,

- is malleable,
- has a pungent, earthy aroma.

Arthur was aware of smell's "power to affect the brain emotionally" (Ratey, 2002, p. 65) and hoped it might entice Jeffrey and Georgia. Yet, there was peril: Smell can as easily repel! Such is the challenge in teaching, the risk that your suppositions are wrong.

Pincer Movement. Arthur first demonstrated the pincer movement: "Pinch it. Like this." With great precision he isolated his thumb, index, and middle fingers, brought them together, opened and closed them as a pincer, effectively nipping a bit off the block of clay. The brain reconfigures the same muscle groups that make a pincer so that they hold a pencil. Writing is difficult for many children because they rarely have used these muscles in combination.

> Since any developing grip might be used for power or precision (or some combination) and since the size of the object to which the grip must conform is variable, the thumb may align itself in any of the possible permutations of pronation, flexion, extension, adduction, or abduction. . . . [T]he balanced interplay of opposing pulls and the wavelike flow of forces circling the thumb . . . produce its complex movements. (Wilson, 1998, p. 136)

Eight eyes fastened on the gesture although Arthur had not yet touched the clay. With exaggerated slowness and great drama, he advanced his fingers-made-pincer toward his hunk of clay. Jeffrey actually gasped as Arthur pinched off a walnut-sized chunk. For the next 20 minutes, teacher sat with toddlers as they nipped clay. Derrick immediately understood how to configure his fingers and nipped his own *and* Arthur's clay into a pile of small chunks.

With Derrick engrossed and Jeffrey intent on watching Derrick, Arthur focused on Maria, hoping that if she became engaged, Georgia might. Maria was having trouble isolating her three fingers. Moving his chair beside and to her right (Maria favored her right hand), Arthur took each of her fingers in turn: "You need your *thumb*," greatly emphasizing the word and, using his fingernails, making a fast prickling action on the tip of her thumb. Maria stared at her thumb, fascinated by the sensation. "And you need your index finger," continued Arthur, standing it up and prickling it as he had the thumb. "And your middle finger," standing and prickling it too. "Put your fingers down and you try." Across the table he saw Jeffrey and Georgia imitating: They had the movement down pat.

Maria was still uncertain. So Arthur repeated the process, lifting, prickling, and naming each finger in turn, a bit faster but with the same precision. "You do it," he announced. This time Maria lifted all three fingers, but seemed at a loss for what to do next. "Watch," commanded Arthur. Dramatically, with great emphasis and exact movement, he drew Maria's three standing fingers together into a beautifully formed pincer. "What a great pincer!" beamed Arthur. "Do it yourself." And this time Maria made the pincer, first standing each finger up, then forming them into one tool.

"Now watch," commanded Arthur. Rather quickly this time, he isolated his own three fingers, formed the pincer, then, hand aloft, he worked it, opening and closing the pincer again and again. Three toddlers sat at the table, making and working pincers as readily as children make gestures to send the Itsy Bitsy Spider up the imaginary spout. Arthur would have been glad to leave the lesson at that for the day. But to his surprise and delight, Maria, Jeffrey, and Georgia each drew their clay to them and proceeded to nip off bits, engrossed and facilely making the complex movement.

Arthur immediately returned to Derrick whose pile of clay bits covered his place. "Would you like to nip more?" he asked. "Nip more!" Derrick answered immediately. Arthur took Derrick to the clay bin and brought out another large block of clay. "Would you like to carry this to the table?" He showed Derrick how to place one hand firmly under the clay, the other firmly on top, and hold it against his tummy for extra stability. Derrick beamed as he set the heavy load on the table.

Wire Cutters. At one corner of the table was a wire cutter. These can be purchased inexpensively or made (see Chapter 2). By grasping the handles firmly and pulling the wire through a block, you can easily cut slices. Arthur knew that 24- to 30-month-olds have surprising competencies far exceeding the standard fare offered them, and that using only make-believe tools infantilizes toddlers. He would have predicted Bertie's competence with the tongs (see Chapter 2). He also knew that at this age movement is mesmerizing, especially when it is precise, is complex, and involves real work. Using real tools moves toddlers "toward a more robust self reliance" (Wilson, 1998, p. 289) and gives them status. Believing in infant and toddler competence, Arthur always had at hand some tool that could pose a significant challenge (see Chapter 2).

Arthur firmly gripped the dowels, one in each hand, separated them until the wire was taut, and eyed the bulk of clay thoughtfully to determine just where to

The teacher demonstrates how to use a wire cutter, knowing it will give the toddlers a sense of accomplishment.

Photo by Jennifer Azzariti

position the cutter. Deliberately he lowered it and dexterously cut off a slice about a half-inch thick. Derrick could barely contain himself: "Me! Me! Me!" "Would you like to try this yourself?" asked Arthur (using full sentences at every opportunity). "Me!" repeated Derrick, "Me try 'self." Arthur handed him the tool. Derrick grasped the handles facilely, but moved so quickly the wire dangled. Arthur stood behind Derrick, held his hands on top of the toddler's: "Pull the wire taut now and cut firmly." Derrick beamed as a slice fell on the table: "Me pull!" This time Derrick did it. His slice was not smooth and full, but it was a slice. Arthur left him on his own to slice the rest of the block and concentrated on the other three children.

Learning to Work Clay. In the ensuing weeks Arthur engaged the toddlers in a wide variety of techniques for cutting and shaping clay, observing their efforts, and helping as needed to:

- nip off different sizes and bits using the pincer movement;
- gouge out chunks with fingers or tool;
- roll a chunk into a long, thin cylinder;
- shape a chunk into a round ball by rolling it under the palm;
- pound a ball into a slab;
- lay cylinders in a row;
- assemble balls in different configurations;
- cut slices, chunks, and hunks with a wire cutter.

Materials' Two Lives. Reggio educators speak of the two lives of materials—first getting to know the material and later using the material to execute a plan. Whether blocks, marker, clay, leaves, or pencil, the child must begin with open-ended exploration, a period of many months or longer, learning how the material behaves. As children learn about the material's behavior, they also learn about their own—how to observe, move, coordinate eye and hand.

The teachers at the World Bank Children's Center use clay in novel ways. Teachers make small clay balls, spread clay on the light table, cut a shape from a

Each toddler does something different to a slab of clay with a missing circle.

Photos by Elly Solomon

slab of clay to create a void, or provide small objects to use with clay. Many relationships ensue from toddlers' explorations. They:

- flatten the balls, mound them, put them in the void;
- scrape away clay to let light shine through;
- fill the void, enlarge it, or smush the slab;
- embed the objects in the clay or use them to decorate it.

The toddlers take pleasure in combining or reconfiguring the teachers' arrangements. The teachers take pleasure in the surprising connections the children make and their increasing competence in handling the materials.

As a child shapes the material, the material shapes the child. Provided that she is given the time, that materials offer a challenge, and that a knowledgeable adult is at-hand, first tentative pokes or pulls turn into increasingly refined movements. With artists' clay a child must learn about its malleability, the shapes it can assume, when it sticks together and falls apart, when it lasts. Toddlers will discover their fingers as separate entities, as pliers, shovel, hammer, pincer, or roller. Each action, each response of the material—tiny bits of gradually accumulating information—"contribute[s] to the actions and symbolic enactments which she eventually comes to carry out with the clay . . . , the natural products of intensive exploration" (Gardner, 1980, p. 58).

As these four children's techniques accumulated, Arthur assembled different groups, using Derrick, Jeffrey (who showed real affinity for the medium), and Maria and Georgia (still as a pair) to demonstrate the techniques they had acquired. As their skill grew and they approached the age of 3, Arthur introduced more challenging techniques:

- making more differentiated shapes,
- curving elongated pieces,
- making curves join in a circle,
- making slip by mixing a little clay with water until it becomes the consistency of a very thin paste (children love the process),
- using slip as a form of glue to hold clay to clay.

Arthur always punctuated demonstrations with a short statement about the intent and meaning of the work: "*Watch* as I turn a ball into a slab." Or, "See how high I can pile these balls." By stating an intention, he prepared the children for the time, soon to come, when they themselves would express an intent to make some specific object.

On the playground, in the neighborhood, and at the park, Arthur encouraged the toddlers who were becoming facile with clay to search for real-life examples they could make in clay. He urged them to observe carefully, to notice objects' shape, bulk, linearity, or surface features. Careful observation would prepare them for experiences, also not far off, when they would add detail to their work, combine shapes to make complex figures, and use nature and the built environment for inspiration. These repetitive experiences consolidated their skill using clay.

MOLDING THE BRAIN

While toddlers are learning techniques for shaping clay, their brain is being shaped. Ratey (2002) explains:

> The brain is a dynamic ecosystem. The various neurons and networks are engaged in fierce competition for incoming stimuli. Networks that succeed in processing new experiences or behaviors end up as strong, permanent members of the neuronal neighborhood, while unused networks, cut off from the ebb and flow of information, wither and die away. In effect, the brain's structure becomes the information it receives, and so how it perceives that information determines its future state. (p. 54)

With all this stimulation, the brain must preserve constancy. It does so through its interpretation of stimuli, by using stimuli as instructions to:

* modify levels of neurotransmitters and hormones;
* determine rates of electrical firing; and
* regulate the "chemical excitability of its own neural networks." (Ratey, 2002, p. 55)

Past experience determines the pattern in which neural networks respond. The more frequently a pattern fires, the firmer the nerve assembly becomes. "The brain can be shaped by experiences just as particular muscles respond to particular exercises" (Ratey, 2002, pp. 55–56). As the saying goes, neurons that fire together, wire together.

When we provide engrossing experiences, we shape infants' and toddlers' brains. Clay work is one instance of an engrossing experience that builds the brain. However, this happens only when there is repetition, variation, transformation, and novelty, and when the purpose is joy in the handling, not a product driven by a lesson plan or determined by state standard. In explorations driven by one's own interest and encouraged to continue for as long as interest lasts, children will exceed standards.

Repetition

Doing something once is a bit of noise on the system. It leaves no trace on the neurons so no pattern can become habituated. Remember shoe laces every child once learned to tie? You might show a 3-year-old, but the pattern usually solidified around age 5. Partly, 3-year-old hands and fingers are too new to master such complicated routines. Partly, repetition is essential for mastery.

Interest-Spurred Repetition. Young children love repetition, a tremendous advantage to teachers because if they provide interesting experiences, they usually can count on children's repeating. Through repetition children achieve mastery, literally training the brain. In determining whether an experience is interesting, teachers ask:

- What routines, hand movements, or thinking patterns are embedded?
- What other activities are variations of these?
- What variation might appeal to a child who resists trying or repeating the initial activity?

Repetition-Spurred Hard-Wiring. In the early 1980s neuroscientist Michael Merzenich implanted electrodes in the region of monkey squirrels' brain that is responsible for finger movement, and watched computer images of their brain as they fished acorns from increasingly smaller cups. He saw the responsible area grow as the task became more challenging, then saw it shrink once the task was mastered, and watched lower functioning parts of the brain take over. Others' research showed the same effects in humans. The conclusion: The more we use a neural pathway and encourage certain functions, the more fixed they become in the brain. Once a function is automatic, it becomes *hard-wired*. Once hard-wired, it takes less of the brain's processing resources than while the function is being acquired. The research proved that "cortical maps are dynamically maintained and are alterable as a function of use" (Merzenich et al., 1987, p. 281). Thus, research proved that repetition is essential to habituate any skill. Mastery requires high-level thinking and occupies a lot of real estate in the brain. But, once mastered, a skill is relegated to a part of the brain that requires less attention. In other words, the brain rewires itself. This is called neuroplasticity, today the focus of a huge amount of research.

Repetition-Spurred Learning. The implication for education is that repetition is essential to learn a skill. Some teachers avoid repetition as the enemy of creativity. Some curricula, in an effort to cover more topics, use little repetition. Others use drill/kill lessons for children as young as 4. Any hand skill and formal subjects like mathematics, reading, writing, the humanities, or sciences require students to learn using a combination of thought processes; many are complex alone, and even more so when combined. Few master these alone, but require coaching, guidance, encouragement, cajoling, demonstration of precise methods—and repetition.

Systematic practice involves repetition, redundancy, correction, and praise. Thus, children learn to master skills, crystallize thought processes, and fix them in their brain. In other words, to learn requires repetition over time. In a 2007 lecture, Reuven Feuerstein called lack of repetition "running away"; it is the opposite of a systematic process. Repetition is essential to form neuronal connections. The issue is how to use repetition creatively so the innate love of challenge stays alive.

Variation

Variety encourages repetition, leads to mastery, and is the key to making repetition palatable. Mastery proves to children that they can meet challenges and keeps alive the love of learning that is intrinsic to humans. Variety focuses attention when it:

- isolates a particular facet, action, or meaning, as when Arthur first nipped clay, or Jan (see Chapter 2) used glue as its own material, not to glue some *thing*;
- embodies a clear meaning—clay can be manipulated in many ways; glue feels sticky and makes things bind;
- makes meaning explicit through concrete manipulation;
- uses the group—each child's unique strengths—to foster learning;
- encourages children to relate the experience to something in the past or future.

Arthur's intent was for children to develop the hand skills necessary to shape clay facilely. He varied whether to:

- make pieces the size of tiny pebbles or as large as tennis balls;
- "work" clay by hand or with a tool, and what tool;
- pinch or gouge with fingers;
- roll, slap, squeeze, knead, press between, or flatten with one or two hands;
- join pieces—and what to use to join them;
- mold the clay for the sake of molding or make some specific thing (always, with toddlers, part of a context in which they are immersed);
- finish a piece in one or several sessions.

Clay is intrinsically interesting and the possibilities for variation are extensive. Thus it offers challenges and provides different entry points for children with varied interests, experience, and skill. A challenge for teachers is to find ways to vary any task that requires mastery.

Activities designed by psychologist Reuven Feuerstein require learners "to repeat the same schemata over and over, but each time in new situations that change in level of complexity and/or modality of presentation" (Feuerstein et al., 2006, p. 400). Modality means the form in which something is received or expressed—words, image, music, body language. Humans employ an endless number of modalities. What Feuerstein calls modality, Gardner calls intelligence, and Reggio educators call languages. Changing modality renews interest and thereby entices children to repeat; changing modality may reach children who are mode "deaf."

Transformation

Transformation is the second life of a material. The first is children's initial use of a material to become familiar with it. In the second life they use a material intentionally and transform it to make some "thing." In both lives, repetition is essential for the brain to consolidate learning, in the case of clay, learning the increasingly complicated movements that bend clay to one's will.

There are two kinds of repetition: One, already discussed, is to consolidate and crystallize a skill, as when a toddler trains fingers and hands in the movements necessary to make a clay ball or snake. The other is repetition in order to transform.

> *Brian*, 36 months old, making a long clay roll: "Now it's a snake."
> Cutting the roll in two pieces: "Now it's two snakes." Reshaping one into a V: "Now the bird caught the snake."
> His teacher *Marlene*, realizing that transformation is a powerful brain function: "You just made a story! Would you like me to tell it to you?"
> *Brian*, head bobbing up and down: "Tell it to you."
> *Marlene* began: "The clay hunk became a clay snake; the clay snake became *two* clay snakes; one clay snake became a bird. Would you like to tell the story?"
> *Brian*, repeating: "Clay became a snake; snake became a bird."
> *Marlene*: "Can you tell me another story?"
> *Brian*, thinking for a minute, making the remaining snake into a V: "Now. The bird has a friend."
> *Marlene*: "You changed the clay to a snake then you changed the snake to a bird! What a good story about clay!"

Throughout Brian was busily using his hands to transform the clay and using words to narrate. Transformation, in Brian's case of actions into words, is a higher level brain function in which some aspects of an experience remain constant (in this example, the material) as others change (the material's shape).

Marlene called Brian's attention to the transformation. But, as with tangible materials, intangible ideas need time to gestate. Ideas, like materials, must be manipulated over a long time, repeated, and varied. Marlene recognized when the moment was ripe to label Brian's exploration with the word *transformation*. In time, with explicit teaching, children learn a principle like transformation.

Clay is clay no matter how it is sculpted. Water has the same chemical composition whether it is liquid, solid, or gas. The number 10 has the same value whether it is expressed as $5 + 5$, $1 + 9$, or $3 + 7$. Principles form the rules of behavior for the universe. Recognizing constants, even when something looks different, is evidence of the kind of deep understanding that is the hallmark of learning.

Learning means to be able to hold a rule constant in spite of conflicting perceptual information and to apply the rule to progressively new and varied applications of an initial task. Because children are rarely engaged in experiences in which they learn about transformation by manipulating concrete materials, they neither recognize, master, nor consolidate its principles. The aim of education is for children ultimately to apply many different principles to many different situations or, in other words, to think flexibly and adaptively.

Novelty

Generally we become bored when there is no novelty. Novelty is necessary to keep the brain's reticular activation system alert (see Chapter 2). If repetition is purely mechanical with no variation, the brain becomes bored. The brain constantly requires novelty to be ready to function. Yet, dull rote lessons are the mainstay of school instruction. Because they lack novelty, they elicit limited mental activity. Novelty makes the brain conscious of an activity and stimulates the capacity to act flexibly. Conscious attention and flexible actions help to crystallize information so the brain consolidates what is learned and stores it in memory.

Memory

Without repetition, variation, transformation, or novelty, the thing to be learned may remain merely an episode. It is rarely possible to hold an episode in memory and therefore impossible to transform it into concepts, to generalize it, or to make abstractions from it. Kenneth Craik (1914–1945), one of the earliest practitioners of cognitive science (tragically killed in a bicycle accident at age 31), saw the study of psychological and physiological mechanisms as fundamental to an understanding of mind. He understood: "You cannot wring the truth out of a particular observation of a particular event" (Craik, in Collinson, 2002). Doing something just once, a single episode, not fixed in memory, leaves no basis for forming new, more adequate thinking. *To learn, a child must see the principles, rules, natural laws, behavior of materials, content—or whatever is being presented—in operation across diverse phenomena.*

Reggio Productions

Children in Reggio infant/toddler centers use clay enough to remember hand and tool movements. Thus, as they turn 3, 4, and 5, their work becomes increasingly complex. They produce remarkable sculpture because of their long, self-motivated use under the guidance of teachers who calculate how to develop the aesthetic sense and to challenge cognition.

Being asked to make "things" from a particular material before they have the skill can kill children's desire to use the material. The question is how to slow down. When Mattie's teacher observed the baby's hesitation, she simply engaged Mattie in rocking the clay back and forth. That simple, un-clay-like activity enabled Mattie to develop a shoulder/arm/hand routine and gave her skin/brain the sensation of how clay feels. In that unhurried introduction the infant found her own comfort level, had a pleasurable experience, and fixed sensations and processes in memory. Repetition, variety, novelty, and pleasure habituate actions and form memories. Because these processes are an inextricable part of Reggio experiences, Reggio children produce complex work.

JOYFUL TACTILE EXPERIENCES

The instinct to touch is pervasive, and touch is the only sense that provides actual contact with the physical world. Even into adulthood the development of the brain and its expansion are influenced by touch. Among the senses touch develops first and in newborns is more fully developed than sight or hearing. Dr. Edward Perl, the pioneering neurophysiologist who established that pain *is* a sensory phenomenon on a par with sight, hearing, taste, and the other senses, said: "When you watch a baby touch, you are watching the development of intelligence in his or her cerebral cortex" (in Ratey, 2002, p. 76). Touch is prominent in the infant's first weeks. It is evident in the rooting reflex and locating the nipple when nursing (Ratey, 2002).

The activities described here with clay and the activities in Chapter 3 are highly stimulating to infants' sense of touch. Autistic children may have extreme sensitivity to touch, their brains unable to process information from tactile stimulation because it may cause actual physical pain. Toddlers who resist wearing certain clothes, run screaming when their mother approaches with a particular shirt, or rip off a piece of clothing were once considered *difficult*. Today we know such reactions *might* indicate autism and we can respond not by scolding, but by removing the offending article or restructuring the environment or experiences so the child is not overwhelmed by stimuli his brain cannot process (Ratey, 2002).

The skin, through which we touch, is the largest sensory organ, and if stretched out would be about 2 square yards. Its processing takes place in three ways:

- direct stimulation of the skin itself;
- knowing where the body is and what parts are moving or still;
- knowing how internal processes, like breathing or heart rate, are functioning.

With 100 receptors per square centimeter, far more than anywhere else on the body, the finger tips are a primary way to identify objects. Michael Merzenich's research with monkeys showed that when the tips of the three middle fingers were used for extensive touching, their tactile sensitivity increased. After several months of training, corresponding areas in the somatosensory cortex (the part of the brain with maps of all the body's tactile functions) also expanded (Kandel, 2006). Research on the hands of musicians and nonmusicians, as well as musicians whose hands perform different functions, shows "dramatic changes in cortical maps as a result of learning" (Kandel, 2006, p. 218). Changes occur daily in the brain, "a minute bit at a time" (Ratey, 2002, p. 86) in response to stimuli. Change is a highly interactive process and, when viewed in action with PET scans or fMRIs, provides an amazing glimpse of how the brain learns (Ratey, 2002). Teachers can offer a material like clay as an input to the process of change, and they can observe what children do as the output of the process of change. But until we bring the technology of PET and fMRI scans into the classroom, the process of elaboration—what happens in the brain between input and output—can only be intuited.

CONCLUSION: CLAY, CREATIVITY, AND COMPETENCE

Today we understand that every brain function is extremely complex, every brain is different, and infants and toddlers organize their brain through experience. Materials' diversity and versatility offer teachers a wealth of opportunities to provide new experiences. The cautions are to repeat, as Arthur did with Derrick, Jeffrey, Maria, and Georgia; to go slowly as Mattie's teacher did; and to honor each individual's reaction. Then children become comfortable and the brain has time to build new circuitry. "Scientists believe that appropriate stimulation of the brain is *critically important* during periods in which the formation of synapses is at its peak. It is during these critical periods that a child's experiences can make the most difference" (Berk, 1994, p. 2, emphasis added). The years 0–3 are such a time.

Infant/toddler teachers have the responsibility, challenge, and pleasure of providing stimuli and observing reactions. As children master new challenges—with clay as with any other material—teachers observe the processes of a brain in formation and of children's using the brain's diverse capacities creatively and with increasing competence.

7

Mark-Making

All children will learn the joy of drawing if . . . [adults] refrain from the well-intended but deadly use of qualified criticism or excessive praise during the very early, very critical, very creative years of childhood.
—Chuck Jones, Creator, Wile E. Coyote, Road Runner, and . . .

Among many ways that the work from Reggio infant/toddler centers has opened our eyes to children's competence, mark-making may be foremost. It is a daunting medium because we hold iconic images: Leonardo da Vinci's sketchbooks; Albrecht Durer's violets; our era's Chuck Jones, whose inventive hand suggested Wile E. Coyote's and Road Runner's nefarious motives with a flick of a pencil. Once, in the late 19th and early 20th centuries, drawing was considered an essential part of the curriculum, and the ability to render a reasonable likeness was considered an important skill. Now drawing, if used at all, is rarely in the curriculum outside the art room, which itself is allotted only a bit of children's time. Yet, mark-making is as innate to children's development as it is to our species' evolution; it is essential in many professions, and it is useful in clarifying an idea.

I was reading to Sheppy, age 4, and the word *dinghy* came up. To explain it, I drew a very simple outline of a coast with a narrow inlet to the sea and at the entrance of the inlet a ship with a dinghy hanging on it. "Could the ship enter here?" I asked. "No," answered Sheppy, "but the dinghy could." Two weeks later his grandfather, a boat owner, told me they had spotted a dinghy and he had asked Sheppy if he knew what it was. "Look, grandpa," he said, taking a pencil and paper, and proceeded to reproduce my simple drawing and use it to explain to his astonished grandpa what a dinghy is. Drawing is a wonderful explainer (even if, like me, you can make only the simplest of sketches).

In this chapter I briefly recap the developmental path of drawing, describe the importance of drawing in Reggio practices, and show the relationship between drawing and critical thinking.

A NATURAL LANGUAGE

Mark-making is as natural a means of expression as spoken language, and they develop simultaneously. Mark-making helps children acquire a sense of self-worth

A 16-month-old uses either end of a paint brush, more interested in the movement than in making marks.

Photo by Ann Lewin-Benham

and develops keen observation. Here I describe how mark-making conveys meaning, how it is a maturational imperative, and what the teacher's role is in provoking children to make marks.

Marks and Meaning

Drawing is more precise than speech: A child can say, "The engine makes the train go," yet have no sense of the relationship between the engine and the train's movement. But, if he draws the engine making the train go, he must make some sort of mark to show the relationship. Then, a teacher can engage him in conversation, point him to pictures or diagrams in books, search for simulations online, and find the stimuli to help him learn more about the actual relationship. The marks young children make reveal how they are thinking.

An infant first may use a paintbrush by making marks with the handle end, not the brush. The *movement* interests him more than the mark. Some teachers use paint for early mark-making experiences because children cannot help but notice it. Two-year-old toddlers mark any surface at hand with excited bursts of scribbles. Three-year-olds make a huge diversity of forms that appear geometric; one is recognized by many who study young children's drawings for its resemblance to a cross inside a circle or square. The development of drawing is predictable—"marks, forms, objects, scenes, and fledgling artistic works" (Gardner, 1980, p. 6). Gardner finds it amazing because the child has not been shown how, yet "each normal child, progressing at his own rate, seems to go through just this sequence" (p. 6). Drawing by children under 2 years old is devoid of symbolic meaning and reflects motoric imperatives.

Sheppy's teacher gave him chalk with black paper when he was about 18 months old, taking the chalk out of the box for him. He was familiar with soft materials—paint, bristles, play-dough—and looked beseechingly at her for an explanation of this rigid stick. First he rolled it, as he had play-dough; it neither "gave" nor left a mark. Then he took a piece in each hand. He made a few random lines, not intentional, hit the chalk on the paper in time to music that was playing,

Chalk puzzles this 16-month-old who has used only malleable materials. The action of fitting the chalk in the box holds his interest longer than using the chalk.

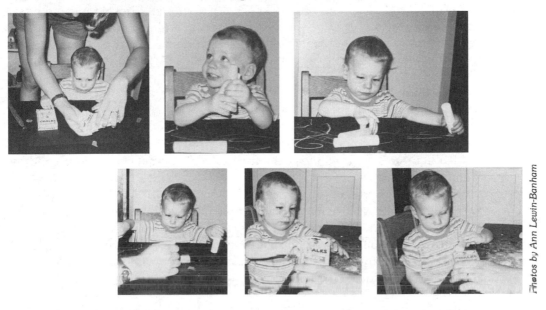

watched as his teacher made some marks, smudged the chalk dust that had fallen on the paper, and was done. Putting the chalk away was a bigger experience than using it, and he focused intently on the act of inserting the chalk into the box. At the Model Early Learning Center (MELC) we used chalk on a huge vertical board, 8 feet wide by 4 feet high. For children under 3, moving the chalk in the large space was the experience. Zen at age 3 loved to draw. Her pencil marks, indistinguishable even with her narrative, accompanied long stories: "This is wind blowing in the sky . . ." She took no notice of the fact that her mark-making bore no resemblance to her narration.

This verbal almost 3-year-old moves the pencil to accompany a long story she is narrating about the wind with no idea (yet) of using her marks to represent some "thing."

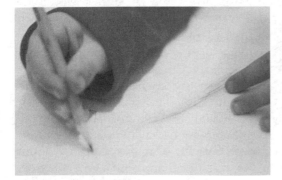

Photos by Alexandra Cruickshank Photography

A Maturational Imperative

Two hundred years ago no one knew about stages of development. Today, every parent watches eagerly for the first smile, intentional coo, and sitting up, aware that each is a milestone, relieved if firsts occur when experts say is typical. Yet mark-making is not on most lists of "firsts." It should be. It is as strong a maturational imperative as walking or talking and involves as many complex brain functions.

Writing in 1980 Gardner saw an "emerging consensus" that the child's earliest marks result from enthusiastic movement—banging, swooping, pulling. At some point the motive becomes visual, spurred, perhaps, by the child's noticing a dark line on a light surface. Then the geometric forms begin that characterize children around the age of 3.

Were this book to go beyond year 3, we would watch mark-making become patterns as children establish "a vocabulary of lines and forms—the basic building blocks of graphic language" (Gardner, 1980, p. 11). Between children's third and fifth year we would see recognizable drawings. And even these evolve in fixed archetype-like patterns: the emblematic sun in the upper corner, green line for grass, blue line for sky, rectangle for a house with crosses for windows (Gardner, 1980).

> Consider a 23-month-old's "scribble:" What is probably most striking about this image is the speed with which it was created. Children of this age often secure what might be called "action pleasure," . . . derived not only from the rapid movement of hand, arm, and wrist, but also from the visual properties that emerge from the action. In a sense, drawing becomes an event rather than an intentional effort to delineate the features of some object, situation, or person. (Eisner, 2002, p. 103)

Gardner (1980) describes a child just under 23 months who in under 10 minutes in a "heated frenzy of scribbling" (p. 25) produced 2 dozen drawings. It was the natural movement of arm and wrist that produced the schematic ovals from circular wrist motion, the dots from jabbing hand motion, and "intricate writing-like forms made by a marker grabbed tightly in the fist and twisted back and forth" (p. 32). These do not represent cognitive activity like imagining and planning. Rather they are "impersonal developmental forces, the stuff of growth itself" (p. 33). In the first 3 years the child has effortlessly established the building blocks of speech, its phonemes (sounds), and morphemes (smallest combinations of sound that convey meaning). Gardner (1980) calls phonemes, morphemes, and a vocabulary of line and shape "building blocks . . . meaningful, referential units" (p. 11). If you intervene when a child of this age is playing, drawing, or discussing, it might break a concentrated act. "The youngster is immersed in a world of his own making, one of tremendous creative significance, but one that can be readily dissolved" (p. 33). Gardner sees a relation between early drawing and other concurrent developments: Markers correspond to other tools the toddler is beginning to use; drawing of enclosures that resemble circles or squares correspond to his efforts at categorizing everything that is new. But we cannot "find a final—or even a first—cause for what is intrinsic to the processes of development" (p. 37).

Teachers' Role

Physicist/philosopher/educator David Hawkins in his seminal 1967 essay "I, Thou, and It" says that the teacher's role (I) in combination with child (thou) and tool (it) is:

> to provide a kind of external loop, to provide selective feedback from the child's own choice and action . . . to respond diagnostically and helpfully to a child's behavior, to make . . . an appropriate response which the child needs to complete the process he's engaged in at a given moment. . . . The teacher . . . [thus] adds to and in a way transforms the interest the child develops spontaneously. . . . The first act of teaching . . . is to encourage engrossment. Then the child comes alive for the teacher . . . [and] the teacher for the child. They have a common theme for discussion, they are involved together in the world. . . . The richer this adult-provided contact [the *it*] . . . the more firm is the bond that is established between the human beings [the *I* and the *thou*]. (1974, pp. 53–59)

Herein lie two lenses through which to look at the following description of a Reggio infant/toddler project that includes representational drawing by toddlers under 3. One lens is understanding that drawing is a maturational imperative; the other is understanding the relationship among child, teacher, and experience. Experience encompasses environment, tool, marker, block, or any other objects or materials. Reminder: Reggio educators are exceptionally good documenters. So effectively do they capture minute gestures and significant expressions of children's actions and words, that their role as documenter becomes invisible. Thus, as you read about the experience called *Little Ones of the Silent Pictures* (Malaguzzi, 1991), understand that you are looking at children's "engrossment" and also at a teacher—indeed a culture of teaching—who has:

- consciously and with great exactitude established an environment,
- filled it with potentially engrossing objects,
- stood ready to observe and to intervene (or not intervene, a conscious choice) at every moment in children's involvements,
- encouraged engagement that at times is spontaneously chosen by the children and at other times provoked by the teacher.

These features provide the structure in which the following experience took place.

A STORY FROM REGGIO

In Reggio infant/toddler centers we see drawings by very young children. The one that appears in the book *Little Ones* is a composite by children ages 2 years 5 months to 3 years 1 month. It is recognizable as a sea of fish. The book documents the project that spurred the drawing.

The Life of a Project

The project began when the teacher read a board book that contained simple, colorful illustrations of fish. Every day thereafter, sometimes with the teacher, sometimes among themselves, the toddlers poured over the book. One day their teacher took two children on a walk, "so young that they have not acquired words and . . . [their] stride [is] made clumsy by diapers and jerky by the laws of gravity" (Malaguzzi, 1991, p. 14). They returned with a goldfish, and an adventure began in which fish and toddlers made friends, and children's faces pressed for long stretches against the tall glass fish bowl, holding discourse. Their conversations were a "submerged and silent laboratory of attempts, trials, experiments in communication" (Malaguzzi, 1991, p. 14). They fed the goldfish, put it to bed, told it "Ciao!" They enacted imaginary scenarios with paper fish on sticks that they maneuvered against a shadow screen.

One morning the teacher introduced a huge fiber shell about 5 feet long with a big foam rubber fish inside. The children played, making the big foam fish chase the little paper fish. The games became more daring. A child plunged the foam fish into the goldfish bowl! This was too much! One of the children grabbed the foam fish, raced to a balcony, and hurled it to the ground. But another child, sensing that everyone was upset, ran downstairs and saved the foam fish. So, the adventure resumed "in cheerfulness and noisy merry-making of hugs . . . reuniting the children, the foam fish, and the goldfish" (Malaguzzi, 1991, p. 14).

At the end of the book discussed above are the composite drawings of fish by 17 children. These drawings are not the first time they have used fine-point markers, but may be the first time they have made drawings that represent an object. Each individual fish shows that these toddlers can use drawing for intentional purposes.

Toddlers from 2½ to 3 years old in a Reggio infant/toddler center drew with every intention of representing fish.

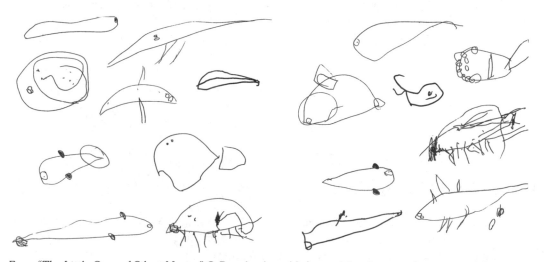

From "The Little Ones of Silent Movies" © Preschools and Infant-toddler Centers—Istituzione of the Municipality of Reggio Emilia, Italy, published by Reggio Children, 1996.

A Context for Drawing

Typically, 2½- to 3-year-olds' first enclosed "things" are tadpole-like figures that children identify as people. All the more wonder that the Reggio toddlers' fish resemble fish. What prompted these likenesses, made not just by one but by all 17 children? Reggio educators, as we will see here, immerse children in experiences through which they come to know things deeply. Toddlers draw only *after* they have had many related experiences. In a typical early childhood center a teacher might read a book about fish, discuss it a little, then pass out paper and tell the children to draw fish. In contrast, Reggio toddlers' experiences might continue for weeks or months, their drawings emerging along with the experience.

Experiences. In *Little Ones* the toddlers began with a book, then moved to experiences with a real fish, one they purchased and lived with as a friend for many weeks, playing an intimate role in its forays through its tank and its feedings. Next followed dramatic reenactments in which teachers used the classroom's shadow screen. (Every Reggio classroom has a shadow screen.) The children *became* fish using paper facsimiles the teacher drew, cut, and mounted on short handle-like sticks. Shadow play with teacher-made props is a regular part of life in Reggio classrooms. By means of a strong light and lens, small images became enormous, shrank, and enlarged again and again as children moved toward or away from the light source.

The teachers orchestrated endless possibilities for encounters among children and fish. Some children "swam" their fish as others watched the show, actors and audience freely changing roles. Such play can continue for weeks. I observed a class at Il Girotonda Infant/Toddler Center where shadow play with fish, also inspired by a book, had gone on for an entire school year, also using rich play with "fish" props before and behind a shadow screen. "The toddlers . . . had become so involved, they were preparing a year-end show for their parents" (Lewin-Benham, 2006, p. 81).

Big Experience. A teacher in *Little Ones* caused an extreme occurrence. Suspecting that something dramatic might follow, she introduced an enormous auger shell, hollow inside. Perhaps she happened upon the auger, recognized its relation to the children's fascination with fish, and used whatever means of purse or persuasion was necessary to acquire it. Perhaps she collaborated on its creation with Mariano Dolce, the resident Puppet Master, whose talents serve dramatic ends in all 50 Reggio schools. Maybe the auger was a department store prop. The importance is not where or how she acquired it, but the connection the teacher made between this item, decidedly atypical, and the children's activity. The teacher went far beyond merely bringing the huge prop: Setting up a potentially dramatic situation, she hid a foam fish inside, 8 or 9 inches long, considerably larger than the goldfish that had become the children's friend. Made of dense foam the fish would withstand water as a stuffed fabric fish would not.

Did the teacher foresee that the children would plunge the foam fish into the goldfish tank? I doubt it! I would guess that she was as surprised as the children—and ultimately the readers of *Little Ones*—when a child grabbed the foam fish and with great force dove it into the goldfish's home, an intentional act with a motive that remains a mystery.

Anticipated or not, the foam fish occasioned an event fraught with peril because the attack could, in reality, have killed the pet goldfish. And the babies—for 12- to 18-month-olds are still babies—reacted with the range of emotions such passionate acts evoke—anger, fear, shock. It changed the entire tenor of their play. This was not a made-for-school activity such as you find in published curricula or in lesson plans drawn to meet standards. Rather, it was a real-life happening, an unanticipated one-time-only set of reactions—the plunging, the shock, the hurling of the foam fish as far from the schoolroom as possible. Yet, the event evoked not only anger. One child, filled with empathy, saw how the action had turned the crowd of congenial friends into an angry gang of many against one.

A Culture of Empathy. We can speculate other directions the play might have taken. Were the toddlers immersed in the 4 or more hours per day of TV drama that is the norm for many toddlers, they might have been anesthetized to the brutality of plunging the foam fish. But, these toddlers did not spend hours watching cartoons, news, and the other media that extend the reality of attack/kill behaviors into our most intimate spaces and make them seem normal. Rather, the protagonists in *Little Ones* resided in a school community with core values of relationships, friendships, attention to feelings, and empathy. Teachers intentionally shared these values with families during long meetings when teachers and parents discussed mutual concerns for children, ideas about development, and the meanings of the children's activities. The value placed on friendship was also emphasized through many conversations among teachers and children, some carefully orchestrated, others spontaneous. Values were evident in the teachers' involvement in the toddlers' play. The purchase of the goldfish was calculated to build feelings of friendship and empathy. So, when the thoughtfully nurtured conviviality of their relationships was threatened, we should not be surprised that a child rushed to restore it.

Conversation and Documentation. The book *Little Ones* does not show everything. Conversation is not shown; yet it is a bedrock of Reggio experience—the gathering of a group before an event to discuss what *might* happen, and the revisiting (through thoughtful documentation of the experience) of what *did* happen, what it means, and what might happen next. Documentation is not shown; it too is a bedrock. It involves selecting children's words and photos that tell the story of an experience and mounting those words and photos on large panels that are hung on a classroom wall. There the documented experience becomes a topic of frequent conversation and reflection as teachers lead children to discuss what was going on, to recall, and to rethink.

Teachers use documentation to spur conversation among children about what they might do next, to take an experience in a new direction, to build new relationships from what catches their interest or sparks their imagination. Drawing, like the composite of many fish in *Little Ones*, is one of many ways that toddlers in Reggio infant/toddler centers relive and better understand what they have done during their immersion in a surround of rich experiences.

COMPLEX INTERSECTIONS: DRAWING AND DECISIONS

To draw something that represents a real object or living thing requires transforming a thought process into action by moving in a particular way. Continually increasing evidence shows movement as a critical part of every brain function—language, emotion, memory, and learning (Ratey, 2002). The implications for what we do in infant/toddler centers, preschools, and the early grades are staggering.

The Brain and Decision Making

Drawing requires split-second decision making: choosing drawing instrument and paper; configuring the hand; reconfiguring fingers, hand, arm, and shoulder for every move the hand makes; deciding when the drawing is "finished" so the hand must stop. Decision making, like memory, draws on many brain processes "all grounded in motor functions . . . [and] precisely the brain regions that guide . . . the motor cortex" (Ratey, 2002, p. 149). To create a new plan, the prefrontal and frontal cortex string together:

- bits of data,
- various actions,
- different behaviors,
- timing sequences.

"The brain circuits used to order, sequence, and time a mental act are the same ones used to order, sequence, and time a physical act" (Ratey, 2002, p. 149).

The wisdom in the Reggio Approach is that it engages children, from the youngest ages, in complex acts that require movement and involve decision making. Teachers involve children in every step of a process. When they draw, they choose paper and drawing implement. If the teacher makes the choice, she has a reason. Maybe she suspects that she ultimately will use the drawings in constrained space. Perhaps they will become a book so she chooses small paper, looking ahead to assembling drawings with text. Images for a book must reproduce well, so she chooses thin-tipped markers that leave a dense, fine line. The logic of a project determines whether the teacher or children choose.

Drawing as a Mental Process

The child making a drawing must access schemata, the word psychologists use for the way the brain organizes and represents something to itself. The brain does not hold little pictures in a "mind's eye," but stores images in ways that look nothing like the object or occurrence in the real world. Pinker (1997) says the toddler's mind contains optical analyzers, motion guidance systems, simulations of the world, databases on people and things, goal schedulers, and conflict resolvers. Drawing requires a child to use all these complex systems simultaneously.

In 1980 Howard Gardner said that at 18 months a child "has not a glimmering that his marks can stand for objects or events in the world" (p. 24). Yet, 6 months later she will. There is no doubt that the toddlers who drew the fish knew they were drawing the same creature that they looked at in the book, "talked" with in the tank, and protected from the foam fish. Malaguzzi (1991) said:

> Children are born "speaking" and speaking with someone. The fact that words are lacking for a year does not stop their insuppressible, vital, eager research to build conversational friendships. The strong desire to communicate is the basic trait of children. (p. 14)

Reggio educators immerse the youngest children in big experiences, observe them, and "listen" to their responses. What teachers see and hear are clues to what connections the brain can make and which of its many systems a child might (or might not) be using. Drawing shows how the brain's eye/hand nexus is working, along with its huge databases, timing mechanisms, and capacities for planning. If you listen to the words of toddlers who talk continuously as they draw, you will hear some of the information in their databases. If you watch them, you will see what relationships they are making between the experience at hand and the schemata in their brains.

SMALL CHOICES/LARGE IMPACTS

Carlina Rinaldi (2006), pedagogical director of the Reggio schools, says listening is a "reciprocal" process (see Chapter 3). Here we watch teachers' reciprocity listening to toddlers in *Little Ones*.

Teachers Who Listen

Repeatedly reading the same book, selecting a particular bowl, or acquiring a new goldfish may seem like small acts. But in toddlers' lives they are enormous.

Which Book? Which Bowl? Why? From the beginning the teachers were fully aware of the infants' deep interest in the book on fish. The teachers "listened" to this interest by returning to the book again and again. They felt no pressure to move on to another book, to "cover" a specific list of books, or in any other way to divert the children's attention from the book on fish. Moreover, they "listened" by making sure the book was visibly and motorically accessible, placing it on a shelf where the toddlers could see and reach it themselves. They "listened" by changing the environment in the most dramatic way: purchasing a living fish, and engaging two toddlers in walking to the store, in selecting the fish, in carrying it back to school, and in emptying it from bag to bowl.

The bowl the teachers chose was itself unusual, a cylindrical vessel about 14 inches in diameter, so large that many children could cluster close at once, so tall that the fish could swim long vertical distances. Paying attention to detail is another way of "listening." It reflects teachers' understanding that a typical bowl would constrain the fish's movements so they would be less interesting. The teachers chose a large vessel where many children could cluster, knowing it would bring different children in close proximity, would foster exchange, and would enable one's reactions to inform and influence the others.

Choosing a Stimulus. Reggio educators are ultimately aware of the impact of new experiences. Many Reggio projects find their impetus in children's reactions to an initial big experience. When you know a fish from the pages of a book, it is magical to find a *live* fish in your midst, as if the book has sprung to life. While observing a live fish might mean little to an older child, it is a source of wonder to a toddler who has never seen one. Reggio educators have a particular talent for constructing wonder-full big experiences. They result from careful listening. We can imagine that the decision to purchase a goldfish and to involve the toddlers in the act evolved from a dialogue among teachers as they debated what experiences might deepen and expand the toddlers' interest in the book. Having two teachers per class ensures that people with different histories interpret from their diverse perspectives the meaning of what children say and do and the implications for what to do next. Additionally, *atelierista, pedagogista*, or Puppet Master—each a specialized professional with no comparable position in American schools—might join the dialogue, adding other perspectives. This group discusses ideas of what might happen next and considers possibilities for branching from interest in goldfish to other interests more or less related.

Bottom-Up Curricula

What Americans call "curriculum" typically is laid out in advance in a program that authorities expect to be followed, often to the letter. In the name of accountability or a mistaken notion of equality, principals or higher level supervisors demand that teachers provide the same predetermined experiences to every child with no deviation. Specialists, who may not have worked with children, design these curricula. Reggio teachers' experience is entirely opposite: Teachers determine from day to day, minute by minute, what to do next based on careful observations of children and thoughtful interpretations of the meaning of what they see and hear.

In service to some notion that teachers must be held accountable, Americans have robbed teachers of the right to listen to children, to use their judgment, to follow their instincts, and to create experiences. Strict adherence to curricula and authoritarian accountability extinguish teachers' thinking and stultify their growth. Teachers in America spend more time justifying how their lessons meet standards than they do observing children, pondering the meaning of what they observe, and engaging in dialogue with their colleagues on ways to respond to what they have seen. Reciprocal listening and bottom-up development are so foreign that most American teachers are at a loss to understand how Reggio educators go about their planning. The small percent of Americans who work in Reggio-inspired schools struggle mightily to cast off training that has taught them to devise lesson plans based on a predetermined curriculum. Those who do shake off this yoke find it liberating and exhilarating to rely on their observations, originality, and dialogues with children as the determinants of what to do.

The yoke is equally hard on children. Throughout life the rate of individuals' development and their interests are highly varied. This is readily seen in pencil grip. Some 30-month-olds, like the girl pictured at the left, already use a good pincer grip. Some use it by 36 months, like the boy shown at the far right. We can see in the photos how his pincer grip has developed between months 30 and 36. Children are more likely to retain their love of learning if they are not forced by a curriculum to perfect specific skills according to an arbitrary timetable. Children in programs like those highlighted in this book have ample opportunities to develop skills in many diverse ways and without timetables.

SELF-PORTRAITS PLUS

Gardner (1980) says that despite diverse cognitive, motoric, visual, and other obstacles, generally around age 4 children draw their first human-like figure and name it—mommy, me, or some other human appellate. Hundreds emerge.

There is great variation in when children learn to use the pincer grip. Some do not master it until Grade 3 or 4. Others never master it. Between 30 and 36 months the boy's grip has changed.

Photos by Ann Lewin-Benham

Children in Zen Rose's class of 4½-year-olds were asked to say what they were thankful for. God, mommy, daddy, and "lots of good food" were typical answers. At her turn, Zen answered: "I'm thankful to live in a house where I can draw whenever I want to." At around age 4

> the various necessary factors—a quiver of graphic schemas, the ability to discern similarities between physical entities and line configurations, the capacity to fashion and execute a plan—have finally come together in a decisive manner, and representational drawing is the inevitable consequence. (Gardner, 1980, p. 61)

Here we watch that happen.

Seeing Oneself

In the 2½- to 3-year-old room of a Reggio infant/toddler center is documentation titled "Noi a tre ani" (Us at 3). A sizable photograph of each child's face, about 6 inches square, is mounted over the child's name. Directly under on paper almost as large is the child's self-portrait; alongside is a verbal self-description, recorded and transcribed by a teacher. Four of the six children's self-portraits are quite remarkable, beyond the tadpole drawings Gardner, Eisner, and others say typify representations of people by children this age. The circle for the head is almost perfectly round. All features are clearly enunciated and include eyes, nose, mouth, and hair, located precisely and well proportioned on the face. Two children added pupils to the eyes, one colored the eyes completely; two added cheeks; one added eyebrows. The circles of the other two are squatter and smaller, and the features less true to form, but they would readily be seen as faces.

At the MELC are photos, self-portraits, and descriptions of eight children who are about 4 years old. The MELC children began school at close to 3 years old, in contrast to Reggio children, many of whom began in the infant/toddler centers. None of the MELC children came from homes with books, markers, or paper; all the families valued direct instruction, especially in letters, over exploration of materials. Yet, four of the MELC children's eight self-portraits are of comparable size, circularity, and detail to the Reggio toddlers'. The other four are far more tentative, somewhere between scribble and tadpole. All the portraits, even those not as detailed as the Reggio portraits, are unusual for the children's age. Yet, any child could do the same in a similarly prepared environment where teachers believe in children's competence and stage experiences accordingly.

Mark-Making "Surround"

At the MELC we nurtured the maturational imperative to make marks. We put paper on clipboards, 5 inches by 7 inches, that, with fine-line markers, we used everywhere, encouraging children to express themselves by drawing as often as by talking. Our Communication Center, where children sent "messages" to one another, was often the first spur to drawing. Children so loved receiving surprises in their mailboxes that they made drawings (well before they began to make letter-like shapes) to "mail." Drawing was fully part of all activities as the means of fostering communication, encouraging precise thinking, and using finger movements that later are required in order to write. The provision of writing centers stocked with attractive pens, pencils, and paper; teachers' encouragement; and other children's examples provided the impetus to draw. As amazing drawings emerged, they provided further motivation. Cognitive growth aside, the children's pleasure in their results was an important benefit. It nurtured imagination, creativity, and strong feelings of self-worth.

While infants were once considered passive, unaware, and a mere receptor of stimuli, an infant's brain—as we now know from neuroscience research—responds as fully, albeit differently, as later in life. The findings indicate that children's acquisition of linguistic, cognitive, and emotional intelligence "is an active process. . . . If infants are in fact editing and processing environmental stimuli, *it behooves us to make these stimuli . . . good ones*" (Ratey, 2002, p. 18, emphasis added).

Reggio infant/toddler centers are models of engrossing environments where thoughtful, caring human interactions envelope children in boundless love and admiration. Simultaneously teachers provoke them in highly challenging ways to make meaning from stimuli. Toddlers take pleasure in mark-making, often smiling as they scribble in random ways or move their arms back and forth across a page, experiencing the sheer joy of movement, barely aware of the visible results. As they gain more precision in hand grasp, they begin to experiment with different types of movement, the results not recognizable to adults as specific objects, except by accident. Usually they begin only around age 3 to assign meaning to their representations. Mark-making is fluid, changing from minute to minute as children "follow the arduous but pleasure-tinged path from sheer random motor activity to patent representational form" (Gardner, 1980, pp. 36–37). Observing them, we see the microprocess of raw development.

CONCLUSION: DRAWING, AN IMPERATIVE

Margaret, teacher of 12- to 16-month-old toddlers, first gave them variously sized and shaped white paper and high contrast black paint with thin brushes, pencils, charcoal, thin- and thick-tipped markers, and oil pastels. She was curious to see whether they would make different marks with different media. They did not. Their marks followed the typical developmental path of drawing regardless of medium—large closed shapes in irregular curved lines; small shapes, some closed, some curved, some open, some straight; marks that looked like scratches; long vertical, short horizontal, and short zigzag lines; a shape inside another; dots; lines and shapes together.

Mark-making triggers brain functions that merge eye, hand, and other networks of neurons, enlarging the ability to focus, sustain attention, plan, analyze, and other high-level cognitive functions that are important components of critical thinking. Often fat markers and crayons are the only tools provided for infants and toddlers. Yet, mark-making is an imperative as strong as movement and language. Therefore it warrants an equal abundance of materials that are varied, provocative, and challenging. It merits the same emphasis as blocks, paint, clay, and other staples of infant/toddler programs. And mark-making exemplifies the trove of ideas that can be sparked and skill that can be acquired when a fertile context nurtures an innate human imperative.

8

Exploring Paper

Now paper is a marvelous material . . .

—David Hawkins (1981)

. . . not only for tempera and calligraphy but also for chromatography, many kinds of model airplanes, miniature houses, and much else. It can be made with a blender and screen from most plant materials and given your own watermark, bound in books of your own binding, or rolled into struts for a geodesic dome. Good books are printed on it, as are good illustrations. But most of these uses are unimagined or forbidden [in school]. (Hawkins, 1981, p. 24)

Philosopher/physicist/educator David Hawkins claimed that everything he knew about children he learned from his wife Frances, an insightful early child educator, who understood how to listen to children and to encourage them to see new relationships in familiar objects as well as to take the perspective of others. Frances's two books and David's essays reflect the culture of teaching and learning that is practiced in Reggio schools, explained throughout this book, and exemplified in David's understanding of potential uses for paper:

The word materials used in school contexts almost always refers to the two-dimensional kind, printed paper. An enterprising group of teachers lobbied successfully for special funds for materials in a more old-fashioned sense . . . then realized their appropriation would miscarry unless they qualified the noun with some very specific adjective. They finally came up with three-dimensional. Paper is really three-dimensional but it gets squeezed pretty thin. (1981, p. 25)

Hawkins's words reflect a philosophy that embodies perspective-taking, the ability to see new relationships in common objects. In mark-making (see Chapter 7) we saw children not learning to draw but drawing to learn. Using paper to foster learning is the subject in this chapter. I show the relationship between the brain's tactile receptors and paper of all sorts, including cardboard. And, I show paper as a provocateur for infants and toddlers to develop new perspectives.

PAPER, BRAIN, AND HAND

We cannot consider paper, or any other material, without considering how the hand moves. As we saw in Chapter 1, neurologist Frank Wilson considers hand function one of life's basic imperatives. Throughout this book we watch infants and toddlers fulfill the imperative for their hands to become competent. Each material builds different hand skills that depend on different neuronal networks. Because paper is varied and flexible, it can broaden infants' and toddlers' understanding about the possibilities inherent in a material and expand their awareness of others' approaches.

"Mentalese"

The brain's representations of actions, words, and images—the "stuff" of thinking—are nothing like the words and images we use. The connections in the brain are so vast, the firing of synapses so fast, that even real-time images—PET scans, fMRIs, or newer techniques to see the brain's white matter—cannot adequately explain brain function. Pinker (1994) calls the brain's representations "mentalese."

> Mentalese reflects a world composed of things and kinds of things and actions . . . , and our mind is designed to find them and to label them with words. . . . Slicing space–time into objects and actions is an eminently sensible way to make predictions given the way the world is put together. Conceiving of an extent of solid matter as a thing . . . invites the prediction that those parts will continue to occupy some region of space and will move as a unit. . . . [L]ift the rabbit by the scruff of the neck, and the rabbit's foot and the rabbit ears come along for the ride. (p. 149)

Actions such as moving toward, reaching for, grasping, and manipulating paper enable infants and toddlers to learn about "things and kinds of things and actions" (Pinker, 1994, p. 149)—surfaces, edges, malleability—and thereby form the basis for mentalese.

Grasping and crumpling fascinate 3- to 4-month-olds.

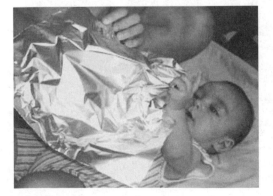 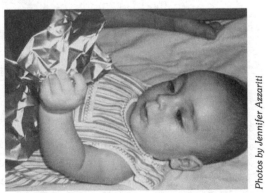

Photos by Jennifer Azzariti

Paper offers stimuli for complex thought processes. Consider these varied ways Reggio *atelierista* Giovanni Piazza describes the "alphabet of paper" and paper's material properties:

smooth, crumple, roll up, fold up, tear up, roll into a ball, cut out, twist, trace, print, wrap up, unwrap, scratch, engrave, place on, take to pieces, reassemble, construct, draw, color, cut, cut up, interlace, wet, soak, punch, bunch, rub out, fit in, duplicate, and decorate. (in Lewin-Benham, 2006, p. 22)

Giovanni also describes movements to make with paper:

hide, sound, fly about, blow, set a fire, set fire to, stand up, cover oneself up, roll, lay down, tread on, mold, paint, graph, chew, bite, lick, and rub. (in Lewin-Benham, 2006, p. 22)

Each requires a highly refined movement. Establishing these "deeply, widely rooted" (Wilson, 1998, p. 10), distinctly different movements is an awesome task that infants and toddlers accomplish with ease. They begin with such seemingly simple actions as "flail," "reach," "move toward," and "grasp." The richer the opportunities for infant/toddler movements, the stronger the brain's neural networks become. Paper is a superb and ubiquitous provocateur of movements that widen perspective as they build hand competence.

Ubiquitous Paper

Papers can come from:

- Kitchen—parchment, waxed, butcher (or freezer) paper; aluminum foil; brown and white bags; muffin cups; shelf liner; napkins; paper towels; contact paper.
- Attic—cellophane, tissue, gift wrap (selected), packing materials, cardboard.
- Office—card stock, envelopes, folders, laminating paper that covers documents like drivers' licenses or paper classroom materials that teachers want to preserve, and chrome coat paper, like magazine covers.

Any papers that have a particular character or aesthetic presence are useful in the classroom.

At the World Bank Children's Center (WBCC) teachers have been learning to use Reggio practices for about a decade. They provide many stimulating experiences, introduce materials creatively, and use diverse types of paper—including cardboard—ingeniously. Contrast their activities with centers where infants lie on their back or are propped on boppies—U-shaped, fabric-covered supports—most of the day, where toddlers watch TV or use thick crayons to color insipid outlines, except when they are being taught letters via drill/kill techniques—a mightily "squeezed thin" perspective, Hawkins might say!

NEW WAYS WITH PAPER: EIGHT MONTHS OF ACTIVITIES

Reggio's influence on the WBCC is evident in the environment—blond wooden furniture, earth tone carpets, soft white walls, abundant natural light, plentiful soft electric light. Children themselves and their work are focal points in the quiet surround. As in Reggio schools, WBCC teachers themselves, not a preset curriculum, determine what activities to do. Watch their use of paper over a 7-month period. In January 2009 two of the nine infants were 10 months old, three were 9 months old, one was 8 months old, and three were 5 months old.

Cecilia and Kristin's Daily Journal

Like all WBCC teachers, the infant teachers keep daily records in a journal, emailed to parents and displayed in a three-ring binder in the classroom. It provides a cumulative record of children's experiences. Here I use entries *only about paper*.

September 23: Firmer-Than-Tissue Paper, First Studio Investigation with Elly. Elly brought two beautiful shades of tissue-like paper, but much firmer, one pale, the other deep yellow. Infants explored its texture, "squnching" it with one hand, trying to mouth it, pulling it with their other hand, listening to it.

September 26: Cardboard Cylinder, Paper Inside. A large cardboard cylinder (stiff, 18" across, 12" high) with crumpled paper inside appeared. The children peered inside the cylinder and managed to tip it when they saw the paper. They listened attentively to the rustling.

October 8: Crumpled Paper Balls. We offered balls of paper (butcher paper crumpled into a 12"–15" diameter "ball"). They grabbed, pulled, held on, tore, shook, and mouthed, as if reacquainting themselves with paper.

Infants are intrigued by cardboard cylinders of all dimensions, alone or with paper or other objects—visible or hidden—inside.

Photo by Elly Solomon

October 10: Stretchy Paper. Elly found an amazing net-like paper, stretchy with regular, small diamond-shaped holes. The infants' faces registered surprise, their bearing intense as they felt the paper stretch.

We also brought cardboard cylinders in again; they patted, grabbed them, tipped them over, and seemed surprised when they rolled with barely a touch.

October 13: Iridescent Paper. Elly brought an array of paper—iridescent, transparent, and shiny—entire rolls that covered our whole bodies so we seemed to float amid a paper sea.

October 28: Thin Crinkly Strands. The children played with mounds of the thinnest, crinkled, green strips. They wound their fingers in it, simultaneously pulling and stretching, playing a long time, 5 or 10 minutes. As they crept, some carried strands with them, wound through their fingers with seeming intention. Others found strands attached to their clothes or hair, the discovery reigniting another round of handling the strips.

October 31: White Paper. The children approached strips of white paper, some long, others twisted. [The teachers found diaper table paper ideal—soft to the touch; firm, but not too firm. It rustles with mellow tones, not the sharpness of slicker papers. It can be crinkled and torn readily by infants as young as 4 months even though their fingers are not strong yet.] Cemetria tore a long strip, then she tore it into smaller pieces, placing her hands on each side and pulling forcibly with her fingers until the pieces became too small to tear. Jarek rolled over and under the paper repeatedly. Sergio crawled away, accidentally trailing a long piece, pulled himself up on the light table, looked in the mirror, and all of a sudden discovered that he was draped in paper. He was fascinated by his reflection—a length of paper hanging over a shoulder, down his back, forming a train behind.

Teachers have prepared a wall of paper, a paper drape, and paper tents, rolls, sheets, and crumpled balls to lure 5- to 8-month-olds.

Photos by Elly Solomon

Sitting in a sea of cellophane evokes different reactions from each of these 5- to 10-month-olds.

Photo by Cecilia Etchegoimberry

November 4: Cellophane. [Cellophane is transparent and glisteny and comes in a wealth of colors. Some are iridescent and the slightest movement makes variations of one tone, as if a blue prism has broken into many shimmering overtones of purples and reds.] We used large pieces of different-colored cellophane and long pieces of brown paper rolled into large tube-like shapes. The infants responded with their hands—grasping, crinkling, waving; then with their bodies—propelling themselves toward, crawling under and over.

November 12: Thin Cardboard Tubes. We brought six cardboard rolls, lightweight, thin, a couple 8 feet long. The infants rolled them back and forth, picked them up, dropped them, reached for them, and crawled over them, quite pleased with their ability to handle such enormously long objects.

November 17: Shapes Hidden Under Paper. We hid flat colored rubber circles under brown paper for the children to discover; once found, they grabbed them, squeezed them, and rubbed their hands over the bumpy new texture. Some spent 2 minutes, others more than 5.

December 2: Cellophane. They grabbed, stretched out the material with both hands, and pushed it together, their crumpling making a fine crunchy noise.

It is a powerful feeling to roll, lift, tip, and push large or long cardboard cylinders.

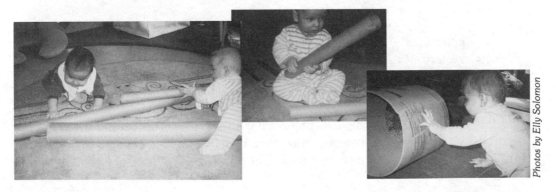

Photos by Elly Solomon

December 5: Large Flat Paper. The most recent time Elly presented leaves, she placed them on two pieces of brown paper. As soon as she spread the paper, the children crawled all over it, trying to find someplace to grab, reaching for the edges. We decided that large, flat paper alone, no leaves, would be a good stimulus. Today as we lowered a huge piece of paper into place, its loud rustling caught the children's attention from across the room. They turned, with huge smiles, as if trying to determine where the noise was coming from. We continued shaking the paper to sustain their curiosity.

Sergio and Akil approached slowly, and we decided to help Ivan. First they crawled back and forth on the paper as if aware their own body was making the sound. When they found the edge, they lifted and began to crumple the paper, which made a different sound. After a couple of minutes they left the area but returned, interest renewed, whenever we shook the paper.

December 9: Cardboard Boxes. We provided a great variety of large transparent boxes 2 feet to 3 feet square and an 8-inch diameter hexagonal box, bright pink. The infants pushed and pulled them, lifted the tops, reached an arm in, and tried to climb or stand in the medium-sized boxes. They manipulated the small boxes more easily and barely used the large ones.

December 30: Long White Paper. The infants were excited to rediscover papers they previously had explored. They shook paper up in the air, uncrumpled small paper balls, tore a long strip into smaller strips, and tried to fit torn pieces into crevasses on the low bookshelf. They made a relationship between some*thing* to stuff, a *place* to stuff, and the *action* of stuffing—object, space, and movement seen from a new perspective.

January 28: Cardboard Cylinder with Paper. Teachers put a cylinder (about 18″ across, 2′ to 3′ long) in the mini-studio, with long white diaper-changing paper knotted at both ends running through it. The toddlers shook the paper and pulled it through until the cylinder was empty, then crawled away. To stimulate a new perspective on the cylinder, we began to play peek-a-boo through it. They played for a couple more minutes, then crawled away. They did not return to the cylinder, but played peek-a-boo through the legs of a chair and from under the platform, imitating us at a distance.

January 29: Cardboard Cylinder with Fabric and Hidden Objects. We continued yesterday's games by covering the cylinder with fabric and hiding objects inside—three clear boxes with materials that make loud noises when shaken—metal jar lids, "jewels" (polished stone-like glass sold for fishbowls), and small stones. Ada reached for the fabric and felt it. Ivan crawled over, pulled the fabric, causing the cylinder to move, and . . . it made a noise! This caught his attention. He pulled the fabric aside and discovered the box inside. Akil and Sergio joined in. Akil fastened his hands on the hanging fabric, swiftly yanked it from the top of the cylinder, and stretched his arm to reach for an object inside. It appeared that Sergio noticed one of the hidden boxes through the fabric and quickly reached for it. We did not know whether he was imitating the other children or whether he discovered the object on his own.

February 9: Acetate and Cardboard. Elly brought acetate rolled inside a thin cardboard tube, which Sergio and Ivan explored [clear acetate called Dura-Lar, see Appendix C]. The boys watched each other closely as they rolled, twisted, and turned the tube this way and that. Meanwhile Elly began to tape acetate, using plain white duct tape, to the mirrored table. The children crawled over and examined the material, more interested in the tape than anything else. When Akil touched the tape, it came off easily. [Edges of this kind of paper tape curl, making it easy both to remove and stick on.] The stickiness completely grabbed the children's attention so we gave them all tape to explore.

February 20: Cardboard Tubes. We repeated the February 9 experience but with larger tubes and paper wound in and around them in different ways. The children became very involved, trying to figure out how to pull the paper out of the tubes while the tubes were upright and trying to unwind the tightly wound paper.

February 27: Small Cardboard Boxes. Materials were received packed in small rectangular cardboard boxes, smooth, white, and sturdy, about 30 in all, a perfect found object. We taped them shut and built a structure on the mirrored table for the infants to explore. They knocked them over, grasped and grabbed them, set them on the table, and watched the reflection in the mirror.

April 9: Long Paper Strips. Inspired by a long strip of cellophane that Sergio brought to school on Monday, we spread many long strips of brown and white paper on the floor. The children explored them with their whole body—creeping, crawling, lifting up strips. They pulled them over their heads, covered themselves, stretched their arms out wide as they pulled hard on the cellophane, and shook each piece, listening to the sounds made by papers of different texture.

April 15: Cardboard Cylinders. The children were becoming more and more mobile, their approaches to the materials still highly individual. They were now using their whole body to climb over or in the big cylinders. Others lifted the cylinders, rolled them, or attempted to wrap other materials around them.

> Motoric mastery is one of the earliest maturational imperatives in the human nervous system. . . . [T]he baby will play [movement] game[s] and rehearse . . . [reach, grasp, drop] movements endlessly . . . giv[ing] itself things to do with its body that are . . . [increasingly] difficult. These games are created by the nervous system . . . to teach itself a concrete, experiential sense of physics. (Wilson, 1998, p. 104)

Infants learn from
handling all sorts
of paper about how
different surfaces,
edges, or textures
tear, crumple, roll up,
make a ball, twist,
pull, come apart, or
dissolve in water.

Photo by Elly Solomon

Neurologist Frank Wilson in his book *The Hand*: *How Its Use Shapes the Brain, Language, and Human Culture* (1998) describes the hand's evolution, functioning, and the remarkable things people accomplish through the hand/brain nexus. The book provides a new perspective on how infants' seemingly random actions build the brain. Its premises make it clear that the WBCC's activities with paper are fostering the maturational imperative for motoric development. Infants' complicated finger actions reflect the brain at work.

PAPER, INFANTS, AND TODDLERS: REGGIO STORIES

Research provides evidence that "infants appear to perceive objects by analyzing three-dimensional surface arrangements . . . object unity and boundaries. . . . [This relates to] physical reasoning (Spelke, 1990, p. 1). The observations of neuroscientists like Spelke, who study the brain in action, help us see the relationship between brain development and the kinds of scenarios that follow. At Panda and Bellelli Infant/Toddler Centers Reggio teachers, with renowned Italian artist Alberto Burri (1915–1995), undertook highly complex projects using mainly paper. The first scenario involves 6- to 10-month-olds. The others involve 18- to 24-month-olds and a few 3-year-olds. The projects are described and portrayed in full color in the Reggio Children publication *Children, Arts, Artists* (2004). All quotes that follow are from that book.

Intention and Research

It was unusual for an artist of Burri's stature to work with infants and toddlers. The teachers approached the collaboration thoughtfully, visiting the artist's studio, and after much discussion concluding that they should record what the children did and the gestures they made *and* should make these traces visible. They began by analyzing their goals, which they concluded were:

- to increase their own awareness of how children explore,
- to learn more about what makes children curious,
- to observe what processes build children's knowledge.

It took considerable time for them to assemble, prepare, and judge the qualities of materials; to weigh their sensory appeal; and to deliberate just how far apart or close together to place them. They chose the floor for the experience because infants spend so much time there. They wanted the children to have a large space, a surprising space that would reveal their "rhythms and strategies" (p. 17).

As Americans attempt to use Reggio practices, we struggle with how to keep and make traces visible and to see and define children's explorations. In the following cluster of projects, called "Blacks and Whites," the teachers keep coming back to the questions they posed to themselves. Reggio educators see themselves as researchers. Their questions are the basis for their research.

Their first question is how they, as teachers, think about the characteristics of materials they choose for infant/toddler centers. A second is how children think about the materials from which everyday objects are made. They felt that choosing blacks and whites was a bold decision since these colors are not often used with young children and sometimes are not even considered colors. In these projects they asked infants to *listen* to the identity of individual materials, only black materials at Panda school, and only white at Bellelli school.

Preparation

The teachers built the infants a black "carpet" at Panda and a white "carpet" at Bellelli. We read these words quickly, but the teachers required days to thoughtfully gather, purposefully choose, and rigorously evaluate the two- and three-dimensional materials that eventually would become the carpets. I suppose designers of typical early childhood area carpets also think about infants' floor time, but with a wholly different outcome: They choose bold designs and loud colors, while Reggio teachers, who look for novel, complex stimuli to the senses, choose subtlety, a chromatic range like going from B to B flat on a keyboard.

The Reggio teachers made no ordinary *carpets*, but a moonscape of textures, pits, and hollows; a lode of crinkles and thuds; a trove of sparkles. The teachers' records show that the children "immediately perceived the threshold," and that "expectations and curiosities drew them cautiously into this new monochromatic landscape" (p. 21). They used their bodies to establish a relationship with the material, altered their posture to investigate more readily, and immersed themselves in exploring the material.

Inspired by such projects, we in the United States want to learn how to ask the questions and create the provocations. Our interest in their work flatters the Reggio educators, but they are so deeply immersed it is hard for them to see, much less convey, the complexity, the time commitment, the philosophical pursuit, and the scientific investigations that drive their work. Like the pundit who observed that the fish did not discover water, we see the Reggio teachers as superb educators who cannot transmit the "cultural water" that nurtures and supports their practices.

Infants' Responses

The teachers' first question was: How aware are we of children's daily encounters with things? Six photographs show the infants exploring the carpets. The striking thing about each is the hand/eye alignment—head intently focused as hand reaches for, grasps, pulls, pushes, feels. The new materials alert the brain's attention system and provoke the hand/eye nexus. Four of the eight infants raise themselves off the floor to better grasp the material.

The teachers had built sonorous, tactile, olfactory, and gustatory stimuli into the carpets. Their second question was: How aware are children of each thing's *essence*? And the answers:

In exploring sound quality, "the children shook, struck, plucked, and pounded to hear rhythmic and sonorous qualities," became quiet with materials that made sounds, and "'talked' to the silent ones" (p. 21). In exploring tactilely, "the children stroked to feel" smoothness, roughness, flatness, whether they were "satiny, puckered, wrinkled," pressing/crumpling, rolling/unrolling, pulling/releasing, testing softness/hardness, seeing "how the material retained traces—proof of their actions." Toddlers who could walk crossed the entire surface, experimented in a "dance-exploration," the rhythm corresponding with "tactile perceptions 'listened to' by feet that are sensitive and intelligent." Infants tasted and sniffed the materials, each using an individual strategy. All spent a long, "almost expanded" time in "alternating rhythms learning: nearing and distancing, entering and exiting, pausing and accelerating" (p. 21).

The teachers' unusual choice of black and white was vindicated by the infants' responses because they showed the ability to perceive "the smallest chromatic nuances" (p. 17). The teachers concurred that the children were equally curious about white and black, found "both colors beautiful [and] recognized their range of shades" (p. 17). The project gave the infants a new perspective on sensory qualities and gave the teachers a new perspective on the extent to which infants are aware of nuance.

Toddlers' Responses

The 18- to 24-month-olds were involved in two projects, gathering materials, then arranging what they gathered into a composition.

Choosing. The children chose from a collection of tones of black and white that included a great variety of materials—paper, fabric, and plastic of different textures, weights, sizes, bulk, consistencies, transparency, and elasticity. Each toddler's strategy was unique, as with the infants, but the toddlers were much more attuned to one another. They worked as a group, others' presence fully part of the learning.

Each child had his own criteria for what he chose: For some it was similarity, materials that would all tear easily. For others it was difference, alternating heavy and thin paper. Some chose without needing to touch, sensing a paper would be lightweight and therefore best for flying. Others chose for texture, using, for example, cardboard's corrugated surface as a piano keyboard. "Explorations were intense, concentrated, aimed at penetrating . . . [the materials'] essence. . . . Hands rubbed, balled up, bent, rolled, crumpled, tore, transformed" (p. 22). The children experimented to see whether they could reverse their effects or conserve the materials' qualities. They tested by aligning, overlapping, bringing together, and rearranging; they were exploring how the materials were juxtaposed. Their arrangements seemed "to show the genesis of composition" (p. 22).

Arranging. The children used different strategies to make their arrangements, as they had in exploring the materials. Some made compositions on a sensory basis—materials that felt soft to the touch when rubbed on their cheek. Others were linguistic, relating a narrative to create a relationship among the materials: "It closes everything," observed Guila (p. 24), who had enclosed "pieces of black fabric . . . in a perimeter of white strips" (p. 24). Some compositions were symmetrical, some random, others unexpected, others beautiful: "I like it the way I put it like that; otherwise it wouldn't be pretty" (Eva, 24 months, p. 24).

"White, White, White" (Alberto, 3 Years)

A common white paper dinner napkin was subjected to explorations by six children. They were a bit beyond the age considered in this book: Giovanni and Cecilia, 3 years; Alberto, 3 years 1 month; Marika, 3 years 3 months; Luca, 3 years 5 months; and an old man, Riccardo, 3 years 9 months. They were exploring an object that is normal, anonymous, assimilated, experienced, habitual. They explored by nose: "It smells good" (p. 28); by fingers: "You can tear it" (p. 28), by air blown from the mouth: "It puffs up" (p. 28); by cheek: "Soft white" (p. 28); and "Like a rug" (p. 28). The children wrapped the napkin in words, using language as a descriptive tool: "Soft like a cat's tail" (p. 28). "It flies up when you blow on it" (p. 28).

Exploration of the napkin continued as children stroked, pressed, crumpled, rolled and unrolled, curled, twirled, folded and unfolded, pulled and released to test the softness, hardness, or rigidity of "an object that is camouflaged by . . . everyday-ness" (p. 27). They began constructing forms. The teachers saw it as the result of earlier experiences connecting "hands, brain, sensation, and material." They folded, wrinkled, rolled up, crumpled, pulled, and tore, and invented descriptive words. Their first constructions were "alphabets, . . . a material grammar that became richer and more complex by exploring fabrics, plastic, and paper in [chromatic shades]" (p. 27). It led to compositions that were formal and varied, allying children and materials. "Each composition bore the personal traces, thoughts, and imprints of the children, and the quality, identity, and peculiarity of the materials" (p. 27). In transforming the napkin, the children alternated between the abstract and the figurative. "It's a snake . . . now it's a crocodile . . .

they're sharks" (Giovanni, 3 years, p. 30). "I put them on white because it [the napkin] wanted the white" (Alberto, 3 years 1 month, p. 31). The teacher noted, "It was often the material itself, reluctant to be modified, that surprised them" (p. 29).

When the teachers judged that the children were finished (how they judge, the teachers do not tell us), they suggested that the children glue their constructions onto a base, square pieces of paper the teachers had cut in the same size as the original napkin, in shades of whites, blacks, and grays. The collaborative work that emerged—25 squares each with highly distinct and complex transformations of the napkin and subtle shades ranging from bright to dull white—would be striking in any exhibit of modern art.

Interpretation

The Reggio educators use many unusual words to describe these children's exploration of materials—material alphabets, dialogues of materials, imprints of the children. They reflect children finding new perspectives in common materials. What is missing, however, is the role of the teacher. She is invisible in the construction. Yes, the teachers selected the material; yes, the teachers "listened," with ears that see in many ways. Yes, the teachers documented the projects so that we can read about them. But what did they actually *do* as these varied constructions took shape? This is what U.S. educators need to know if we are going to move from the kinds of creative introductions of materials we see at the WBCC to the deep explorations we see in Reggio projects.

A primary way Reggio teachers observe is with a camera. They capture hands in split seconds as the hands become increasingly competent in making highly nuanced movements. They "frame" finished compositions by offering the children backgrounds, one per child, on which to arrange their beguiling arrays of forms. They lay out the finished work in a regular grid that they name "the large composition" (pp. 36–37). They interpret the collection as a catalogue, or alphabets of gestures, forms, and mental images. They say the composition is the result of experiments "with resistance, lightness, and delicacy" (p. 29). But the teachers' role in the daily flow of activity—their big decisions and their minute-by-minute thinking—are missing from the descriptions.

Reggio teachers watch how children use words. They search children's emerging linguistic capacity for relationships between thinking and doing/shaping/labeling. They interpret the children's symbolic representations as indications of how they are thinking and of the relationships they are making.

These are examples of teacher collaboration—suggesting the next step, providing a material (square pieces of thick paper) in chromatic tones, calculating how the display will be different in the totality than any individual piece. These are important techniques, but barely enough is revealed to enable teachers new to Reggio practices to follow the thinking, understand the motivation, and adapt the processes themselves.

CONCLUSION: NEW PERSPECTIVES

Whether we eventually land on the right path in our trials to pursue Reggio practices remains to be seen. I hope Reggio practices do not go the way of so many American classroom experiments—tried and found wanting when, in fact, they have hardly been tried. They provide new perspectives on innovative ways to build brain structures and spark children's creative expression. The Dana Consortium grappled

> with the question of why arts training has been associated with higher academic performance. . . . [Their] findings allow for a deeper understanding of how to define and evaluate the possible causal relationships between arts training and the ability of the brain to learn in other cognitive domains. (Gazzaniga, 2008, p. v)

Showing causal relationships is significant.

The WBCC and Reggio schools—rich in experiences with materials, diverse in the media they use—provide examples of how to foster perspective-taking in children. Perspective-taking has two aspects—the ability to see new relationships in familiar materials and activities and the ability to take another person's point of view. This is significant. We see experiences that build perspective in the infant/ toddler rooms at the World Bank Children's Center. We see it widely elaborated in the mature infant/toddler centers that the Reggio educators call *asilo nido*, Italian for sheltering nest. Such classroom events have the potential to stimulate dialogue between neuroscientists and classroom teachers as we try to build bridges from research and theory to practice.

9

Natural Materials

If eyes were made for seeing:
Then beauty is its own excuse for being.

—Ralph Waldo Emerson (1912)

The ginkgos were at their prime, the ancient species lining the long street in intense yellow. Lois took advantage of the bounty, filled a leaf bag, and carpeted the floor of the kaleidoscope as a surprise for the toddlers. The kaleidoscope is a prism, mirrored inside and open on the ends. When children crawl in, they see themselves reflected endlessly. Today children at the Model Early Learning Center would see themselves "engulfed in utter yellowness" (Lewin-Benham, 2006, p. 112).

At the Diana School in Reggio Emilia, the 4- and 5-year-olds embarked on a long, multifaceted project collecting, compacting, and recombining natural materials. The materials the children collected burst with sound and smell. Sorting them into containers intensified their visual, tactile, and olfactory variations. "A palette of colors invaded the space, . . . the material . . . already beginning to weave a story about itself." Because the humidity was different inside and out, color, transparency, and consistency changed. The leaves dried, faded, and curled; the dirt crumbled. The children broke them up further, "crumbling and kneading leaves and soil, [making] a variegated palette, also modified by time" (Reggio Children, 2004, p. 86).

The children's crumbling, crushing, compacting, sorting, and pulverizing yielded over 50 colors. They took this palette of powders outside and used them to *paint* on the ground, in crevasses of bark, between stones, over sand—on every conceivable kind of natural canvas (Reggio Children, 2004). It was called "Natural Materials." The foundation for such explorations is laid from ages 0 to 3.

Zen, highly verbal at age 32 months, had an experience with life and death. Her mother describes:

> We found a millipede in a suitcase. After examining it, Zen made a little home in a box where she put grass and sand. It died within hours and we had a funeral. This was Zen's first experience with death and led to

The millipede is on a mirror. This 32-month-old sees it enlarged under a magnifying loop and also sees her own reflection.

Photos by Alexandra Cruickshank Photography

lots of conversations. At first she asked "Well, when she comes back to life, she will be able to play again, right?" We talked about the fact that we would bury her. In the human tradition of easing grief through mythology, I told her the Scottish belief that when a person dies far from home, their spirit travels back to the land they love, and sang her "Loch Lomond." "Oh," Zen nodded, "so after we plant her, her spirit will go be with her Mom and Dad and her body will become the dirt." A month or so later, we visited a bug zoo that had many varieties of millipedes, a revisiting, in a way, of Zen's experience. She noted their similarity to centipedes and that they were not worms "because worms don't have legs." (Alexandra Cruickshank, infant/toddler teacher)

Nature is a powerful spur to infants' and toddlers' noticing and discussing—everything.

Nature yields a plentitude of materials from every animate and inanimate kingdom—plant, animal, mineral, water, soil. Here I discuss using this bounty as integral parts of infants' and toddlers' experiences. Because color, shape, and texture are predominant in nature, I first discuss vision and the brain. I then describe a philosophy of teaching in which children and teachers communicate with one another about nature. I conclude with examples of how children's intuitive attraction to nature leads to collecting, using natural materials, and sharing their interest in plants and animals with others.

LEARNING TO SEE

The human eye is a complex system made up of equally complex subsystems. In this brief overview, I describe its capacities, development, and functioning.

Capacities

> For at least the last thirty million years . . . the brain has allowed us and our ancestral primates to make sense of the colored world. Despite the skittering of the eyeball, the constant shifts from bright light to shadow in a dappled forest, and the change in hue of the sun from dawn through noon to dusk and sunset, a page like this one is always white, and the leaves of a tree are usually greener than their ripe fruit. The conservation of color—the final interpretive step between photon absorption and color vision—is essential to our sense of the physical continuity of objects over time. Without it we would, I think, go quite mad, or at least wish to keep our eyes firmly shut. (Pollack, 1999, p. 29)

Color is only one of the many facets of a visual system that also enables us to see:

- outlines and boundaries from which we can perceive shape;
- perspective, the relation among objects' distance, relative size, and depth;
- texture and form;
- the most subtle movements, essential for survival in evolution and our deterrent today from hitting joggers as we drive (movement is the source of our amazement at a perfect hoop shot).

The role of texture and form in visual perception is shown in this story of an achromatopic person, related by Oliver Sacks in *The Island of the Colorblind* (1996). Unlike common red–green color blindness, achromatopes are born with a deficiency in the retinal cells that makes them totally colorblind, seeing everything in whites, greys, and blacks. Knut, an achromatope, traveled with Sacks around a verdant South Pacific island. While the color-normals saw just a mass of greenery, Knut saw distinguishable shapes and degrees of light and dark, "a polyphony of brightnesses, tonalities, shape, and textures" (p. 32).

Knut explains how he chose a ripe banana: "We don't just go by color. We look, we feel, we smell, we *know—we* take everything into consideration, and you just take color!" He describes how as a child he would memorize colors of clothing and objects and by doing so was able to learn the "rules" for "correct" use of colors. Through memorization he also learned the "most probable colors" of things (Sacks, 1996, p. 70).

Sight and Neuroplasticity

Sacks says that Knut's unbridled curiosity about color as a child and his substituting memory for perception are examples of how the brain adapts. Knut's adaptation is an example of brain plasticity, the capacity of the brain to continually rewire itself in response to experience. "The brain is all about change. Our individual skills are very much shaped by our environment" (Merzenich, 2004).

Development and Functioning of the Visual System

The visual system has been studied for decades. Pinker (1997) describes its complexity:

> Early in fetal development neurons are wired according to a rough genetic recipe. The neurons are born in appropriate numbers at the right times, migrate to their resting places, send out connections to their targets, and hook up to appropriate cell types in the right general regions, all under the guidance of chemical trails and molecular locks and keys. To make precise connections, though, the baby neurons must begin to function, and their firing pattern carries information downstream about their pinpoint connections. This isn't "experience," as it all can take place in the pitch-black womb, sometimes before the rods and cones are functioning, and many mammals can see almost perfectly as soon as they are born. It is more like . . . a set of internally generated test patterns. These patterns can trigger the cortex at the receiving end to differentiate . . . into the kind of cortex that is appropriate to processing the incoming information. . . . How the genes control brain development is still unknown, but a reasonable summary . . . is that brain modules assume their identity by a combination of what kind of tissue they start out as, where they are in the brain, and what patterns of triggering input they get during critical periods in development. (pp. 35–36)

"The genes build eye-specific neurons crudely and then kick off a process that is guaranteed to sharpen them" (Pinker, 1997, p. 239). We can see because "eyes have precise arrangements of unusual materials capable of forming an image" (p. 156).

- The cornea focuses light.
- The lens adjusts the focus to the object's depth.
- The iris opens and closes to let in the right amount of light.
- The vitreous humor, a clear, colorless transparent jelly, fills and maintains the eye's spherical shape.
- The retina's rods and cones convert images into chemical and electrical signals.
- Muscles aim the eyes up-and-down, side-to-side, and in-and-out. (p. 156)

It is a marvel of engineering, all exquisitely shaped and arranged.

Probably as soon as they are born, infants fixate on face-like patterns, but not on other regular arrangements. By day 2 they recognize their mother (Pinker, 1997). Crucial eye development takes place after birth; many functions enable the brain to make sense of signals triggered by light falling on the retina. There is constant traffic along the optic tract to the thalamus through two large sets of fibers, called the optic radiation, to the visual cortex, which is "made up of billions of cells with billions of interconnections" (Ornstein & Thompson, 1984, p. 113), then to eight other areas for analysis. Information is sent to memory centers and the forebrain for more analysis. "Once the information has been thoroughly processed, checked, and double-checked with thousands of bits of information firing back and forth

Ladybugs are fascinating to infants like this 1-year-old and to toddlers like this 22-month-old.

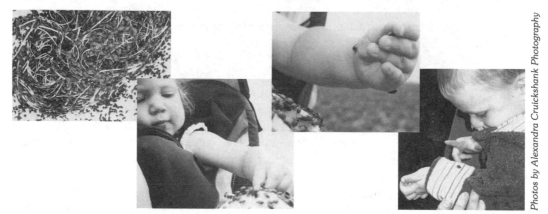

Photos by Alexandra Cruickshank Photography

throughout" (Ornstein, 1984, p. 123), what the eye perceives acquires meaning. Any process can be waylaid by genetic problems, interrupted by birth trauma, diminished by a paucity of interactions, or enhanced by rich experiences. Nature provides some of the richest.

INFANT AND TODDLER INVESTIGATIONS

The brain finds rich nourishment in natural materials. Sunshine makes constantly changing patterns. Rain hits windows and roofs with one medley; birds call with other rhythms and cadences. In one stand of trees are seedlings, saplings, and mature trees—a progression there for the seeking. Skin registers temperature changes from morning to midday, from fall to winter. Ants parade as if organized by a merciless drill sergeant. Spiders capture insects that fall on their web, spinning more facilely than any machine. Smells resonate. Color abounds, each season with its own palette. "Most of us see a world of about two million gradations of color" (Pollack, 1999, p. 26). The teacher connects infants and toddlers with this richness.

Young Children's Pace

Children notice everything—if given time. By 6 months all functions of the eyes work. Sheppy was 22 months. We walked only three houses away, the purpose exploration, not destination. Everything caught his eye—a single ant, an individual floweret on a begonia, a bent twig, a broken bird's egg. If it moved, it had to be watched; if colorful, touched; if detached, carried; if unusual—everything is unusual—its story heard. A large open pile of dirt sent us home for pail and shovel and the walk morphed to a dig.

Toddlers ask for stories in different ways: a pointing finger, a pause, an inclined head, an inquiring look, a question—"Las lat?" (What's that?). Adults read the nuances of the gestures and sounds in these requests. The relationship among stimulus, infant/toddler, perception/processing, and adult response causes further responses from the infant/toddler in exquisite feedback loops. Infants, as we have seen (in Chapter 8), perceive finely nuanced chromatic differences (Reggio Children, 2004).

But, infants and adults have competing imperatives. Adults fill pails to complete tasks. Toddlers fill pails to feel material in their hand, to manipulate a digging tool, to dump the material and start again, to move, to revel in sensory perceptions—the tender greens of spring, the coolness in the dappled sunlight of summer, the aroma of moldering leaves in fall. Adults have difficulty deferring *their* work so toddlers can engage in *theirs*—namely, repeating an activity. Yet, that is what natural materials offer—triggers to the brain's tendencies to repeat, to seek stimulation, to manipulate, to register sensation. In order to make connections, infants and toddlers require a classroom with diverse natural stimuli, access to the outdoors, and an adult with time to listen and observe.

Use of natural materials can start by:

- Following an infant's hand and eye as she feels the grass, grasps a flower, or touches a puddle, and allowing her to explore as long as interest lasts, then moving to a new spot and attending as she discovers different things to see and touch.
- Watching for infants' attention to shadows on a wall or patches of sunlight and holding the infant where she can better grasp or feel.
- Following toddlers' rhythm as they amble over sidewalk, soil, or grass, letting them set the pace, noticing what they notice, and providing names of things and occasional bits of information: "See? The ant is carrying something to eat to its colony."
- Allowing time for toddlers to explore the texture and how a new material moves, and to gather those they perceive as treasure.
- Photographing infants and toddlers as they explore; taking notes of toddlers' words; showing them the photos; discussing their words and actions with them; listening to what they recall; and thoughtfully selecting what to suggest next because you, the teacher, suspect which things might lead down rich paths or which might be dead-ends.
- Looking at books with diverse images of nature.

Using an adult-sized hand shovel to move dirt into a bucket requires a 2-year-old to plan and to master balance, aim, and many other precise movements.

Photos by Ann Lewin-Benham

The finely ground gravel that he has moved, mounded, and gathered is a treasured material to a 26-month-old.

Photos by Ann Lewin-Benham

A teacher's own passions and bits of knowledge are powerful stimulants to children's forming relationships with the natural world. Of these, passion is the more important since knowledge can always be sought.

When Danny was 2½ years old we lived near a small stretch of undeveloped land, a haven for wildlife, plants, and a trove of rocks. One day, he spotted a thin rock, 18 inches long, terminating in sort of a point. This treasure, which he called "spear," triggered an interest. It led to collecting and eventually categorizing, polishing, trading, and studying rocks and minerals in books, at museums, and at rock shows. We scaffolded his "find" with discussions and geologic excursions, augmenting his budding passion with our latent interest.

Hawkins on Learning from Natural Materials

David Hawkins (1983) maintains that "there is more of the basic background experience for mathematics and science in the life of every child than for most other subjects in the early curriculum" (p. 70). Early mathematicians

> drew shapes in smooth sand . . . [and] used just the ordinary Greek [language]; there was no elaborate shorthand [or] symbolic notation such as we . . . force too early upon our children. But from such everyday beginnings, the ancients began to develop some powerful ideas and important questions. . . . Children [can be] guided to do that too. (p. 70)

Frances Hawkins says: "Small children have many more perceptions than they have terms to translate them; their vision is at any moment much richer, their apprehension ever constantly stronger, than their at all producible vocabulary" (in Hawkins, 1983, pp. 74–75).

David Hawkins (1983) cautions that children can speak only of something they have known and that their activities and observations are the best ways for them to remember, make analogies, and generalize. "If the classroom is bare of the materials" (p. 75), there will be no link between what the child observes and states. Natural materials, Hawkins argues, must include illuminations and shadows, plants and animals. These latter engender respect for life. Maintaining life develops both moral imperatives and specific know-how. The "degree of commitment" must be "absolute; otherwise [the plants and animals] die" (p. 77).

Hawkins urges us to investigate how we care for small animals, to prepare a good environment, and to think about food beyond commercial pellets. He describes guinea pigs who lived on

> the grass that was grown on their premises: seeds of wheat and rye and barley grown in their own territory, a large open steamer trunk of vintage 1910, filled with potting soil and peat moss, with rocks and logs and growing plants. They could have left their Eden, but they never did. (pp. 77–78)

I judge the state of my own mental health by the condition of my house plants. If I am depressed, they droop. Classroom animals are also sensitive to their caregivers. Animals will live well only if the children live well. "Otherwise there would be only a surface interest, then indifference and neglect" (p. 78).

As we resurrect the words of this brilliant scientist/humanist, we must beg his indulgence if our present relation with natural materials is mainly pouring glue and paint on pine cones. And, we must commit ourselves to "the concern for human affairs generally" (p. 65), which Hawkins believes is where involvement with natural materials leads. Children are full of latent interests. It is our role as adults to "induce" (p. 65) their learning, to follow where they lead, to revel in the significant things that interest them, things that, without our enthusiasm as a link, *"they might otherwise never gain access to"* (p. 65, emphasis added).

THE BOUNTY OF NATURAL MATERIALS

Holding different plants side by side reveals a huge range of color, texture, and shape. Roots, stem, trunk, branches, flowers, leaves, fruit, seeds, and twigs offer endless and renewable varieties of material. Plant materials can be scrounged free—anywhere. While nature at first glance seems predominantly green and brown, on close inspection greens range from gold to grey and browns from white to black. Leaves' colors on a single tree are chartreuse in spring, kelly green in summer, amber in fall. Leaves change from new unfolding sprigs to mature shapes—willows' and pin oaks' long, pointed leaves; maples' fat, multipronged lobes; sassafras trees' three distinct shapes—oval, mitten-shaped, and three-lobed—all there to be collected, sorted, stowed, and used.

Distinguishing, Collecting

Collecting is a matter of time, observation, bag-at-hand, and teacher passion, with enthusiasm for children's finds. Seeds are plentiful and vary infinitely. The

The toddlers have played in the samaras, gathered them, and watched their teacher drop them. One had the idea of drawing the movement of the seed as it fell.

Photos by Jessica Gagliardi

samara is a flattened wing-shaped seed cover, papery in texture, so the wind can carry it away from the parent. In the elm the seed is in the center, in the maple or ash on one side. Its shape makes it spiral as it falls, giving it the name helicopter or whirligig.

The 2-year-olds at the World Bank Children's Center brought the samaras back to school where Jessica Gagliardi, the studio teacher, dropped them over and over. The children were fascinated by the movement and traced it in the air with their fingers. Adam stared hard at Jessica's clipboard, which she handed to him at once. But he didn't know how to translate the gesture of his finger to mark-making with a pencil. Simon took the clipboard and facilely drew a sort of spiral. Then Carissa took it and drew a zigzag. Watching intently, Adam took it and, this time imitating what he had seen his classmates do, made a line on the paper with the pencil, starting at the top of the page and going to the bottom.

Barks vary. The hackberry, in the elm family, has thick, knobby ridges that protrude like fingers of an old person with arthritic knuckles. Carve your initials and ridges will form. The birch tree's bark is thin as paper (some species are called paper birch) and peels in layers that can be as large as a sheet of paper. These barks are prized classroom additions. (*Caution*: Never strip or peel bark; take only what has fallen to the ground.)

The horse chestnut tree (also called buckeye) has upright flowers, 6 inches long, so the tree appears covered in candles. Its fruit grows inside hard spike-covered shells called conkers—you don't want to be under one when it falls. The fruiting capsules that open in three pods and large five-lobed leaves are large and unusual. Their huge size and candle-like appearance make them special treasures for toddlers to collect. (*Caution*: Don't collect open capsules; the fruit is poisonous. Schools often remove poisonous plants and dangerous tree limbs.)

Bare trees reveal amazing symmetry, intricate networks, and structures that cannot be seen when the tree is in leaf. Some trees' limbs, trunk, or roots assume unusual forms because they have grown around a rock or fence. Others are contorted by severe wind, reshaped by lightning, pruned or shaped by man. The brain's tendency to seek patterns makes us see faces or animals in some of these forms. Children revel in seeking such anomalies. For examples, see http://www.environmentalgraffiti. com/offbeat-news/30-creepiest-trees-on-earth-pics/1381/4

Flowers have evolved in myriad ways to call birds' attention because birds eat the fruit and spit (or s _ _ t) the seeds, which spreads them. Some festoon themselves so beautifully that they co-opt humans into helping them propagate. When children themselves gather natural objects and teachers observe, preserve, and discuss them, long discussions can ensue, augmented by reference books, further walks, Google searches, or discussions with knowledgeable parents, nursery workers, or natural history museum staff to identify finds and learn interesting facts. Once they've become well acquainted with nature's "vocabulary," children can use their hands and various tools to form original compositions of natural materials or to transform them with glue, paint, markers, and other man-made materials. The brain is stimulated by imagining, planning, reasoning, and grappling with the constraints inherent in designing, aligning, and joining different materials. Such interests, which they "might . . . never gain access to" (Hawkins, 1983, p. 65) without a passionate teacher, can last a lifetime.

Using Materials

Rob, an intern, loved nature and, "inducing learning" (Hawkins, 1983, p. 65), initiating or expanding toddlers' leads in different seasons with his class of 16- to 22-month-old toddlers.

Testing Leaves. The toddlers collected leaves, carefully selecting them from raked-up piles. They held, examined, and used different senses to explore and take them apart, testing how they dropped, floated, sounded. Rob cautioned: "It's yucky in your mouth! Just hold the leaf in your hand. Look at it. Put the leaves into the basket." The range of trees in the school's vicinity was limited, so Rob asked parents to find others with their children. The children noticed that some leaves the parents brought were still green after most had turned.

Indoor Explorations. Initially, explorations indoors and out were similar. Crushing leaves happened naturally as a result of handling them. Toddlers would crush for as long as 5 to 10 minutes, then, with Rob, sort crushed piles by color, smell, or texture, and funnel them into containers. Rob and other teachers also crushed leaves for later use. The toddlers were just beginning to manipulate scissors, so they made attempts to cut the leaves. No one was really adept; they handled scissors as if they were a mortar and pestle, prompting Rob to add one to the classroom. Later, toddlers themselves brought leaves into the studio, understanding that materials of all sorts were kept there.

From repeated work with glue, the toddlers realized that it could attach things, and on their own poured glue onto the leaves, more an exploration of glue than of leaves. When offered glue in small paper cups, the toddlers poured in crushed leaves. The glue dried clear and Rob initiated lots of conversation about the appearance and texture. At other times he provided half an inch of glue to "paint" on the leaves. (Glue ruins brushes for other uses. Since brushes are expensive, Rob used cheap watercolor brushes, dedicated for gluing.)

Combinations. Later Rob combined natural with man-made objects, like paint, which is similar to glue because both cover things up. He began by gluing a leaf on painting paper, causing children to use different brush strokes and amounts of paint, to see shape and surface in new ways. Two- to three-year-olds used natural materials in their dramatic play. As with many materials, they became props or backdrops. Taking a cue from the children, Rob encouraged them to bring natural materials to the housekeeping area—pine cones, seeds, wood chips, twigs, stones, shells—where they became cookies, baking ingredients, dolls' pacifiers, kites, swords. In children's eyes, materials are open-ended and adaptable to any role they need. This exemplifies Piaget's observation that toddlers accommodate objects to their purposes regardless of objects' properties. How closely they adhered to cooking or other routines indicated how well they observed and to what extent they were habituating and remembering everyday procedures.

Rob spurred scientific exploration, filling the water table with sand for toddlers to bury, uncover, or combine different natural objects. Sometimes they used their hands, other times tools—cups, shovels, slotted objects, funnels. He also used water, moon sand, dirt, or chips—the toddlers playing for as long as 20 to 30 minutes. As they became familiar with how seeds or twigs behaved in each different medium, Rob encouraged them, "Think about what would happen if . . ." or "Look closely at . . ." or "What does this remind you of?" With water they commented: "It's wet!" "It's cold!" "It's splashing." They also brought props on their own. Rob suggested they add model animals and the play morphed, lasting almost an hour: "My dinosaur is taking a bath." "She's getting a drink." Rob used their imagination to segue to discussions about real dinosaurs, which they explored in many books he added to the classroom and a visit to the natural history museum.

Seeds. Before introducing seeds, Rob held conversations with a group of five children to learn what they knew about plants. Jana, a highly verbal, realistic 31-month-old: "I don't think they'll actually grow. I think they're just pretend grow." Rob poured three different kinds of easy-to-grow seeds—basil, parsley, and oregano, all small and black but distinct—onto three plates. The children were fascinated by the tiny size and talked about the differences.

Jenny, 27 months: "This a black this another black."
Briana, 29 months: "This a turn into a plant; this a needs sunlight, water, and seeds."

As planting began, Rob heard what the children knew:

Glenna, 32 months: "It need a be in dirt."
DeAntario, 34 months: "Dirt a food to a plant."
Rob: "Just sprinkle soil on top. If we pack it . . ."
Chandra, 32 months: "It can't breathe, like when my shirt too tight."
DeAntario, sprinkling the soil very lightly, imitating Rob: "Just a little, it
    like juuust a little."
Shameka, 30 months: "And they need a lotta sun."

The children, considering many places, chose an east-facing window sill. Punctuated with frequent, lengthy conversations and outdoor observations, and augmented by books, the activity continued for weeks. It became prologue for an investigation of how we nurture food sources, a huge topic. Rob saw how closely they observed everything, how germane their own ideas were, and how much content they already had on which to build more experiences. Inspired by Reggio practices, he documented seminal moments in the investigations, gradually building a panel from photos and toddlers' comments, and regularly revisiting the panel with the toddlers to recall and reflect on what they'd done. Next spring, Rob determined, they would start a terrarium.

RESEARCH, NATURE, AND THE CLASSROOM

The idea of fixed stages of development has been discarded because research has demonstrated that the brain is plastic and capable of rewiring to make new neuronal connections. But certain functions have critical periods. Miss them and a function fails to develop. Here I briefly explain critical periods and then show autumn experiences at the WBCC.

Critical Periods

We know today that the brain is highly adaptable, but there are limits. Critical periods are times when specific brain developments take place in fetus, infant, toddler, or preschooler. When these periods pass, the brain prunes many connections, keeping only the most efficient and most frequently used. After that happens, certain functions cannot be acquired (Ratey, 2002, p. 39). Hawkins words echo: They "might otherwise never gain access . . ." (Hawkins, 1983, p. 65).

An example of a critical period is the pronunciation of phonemes from foreign languages. If adults learn a foreign language, they frequently have an accent detectable to a native speaker, and they learn by using different brain systems than the child under age 4 (Spanish phonemes, n.d.). "There is a critical period for social development" (Kandel, 2006, p. 373) and for emotions (Ratey, 2002, p. 42). Some motor and sensory functions also have critical periods. Motor circuits become "hardwired" (Ratey, 2002, p. 41) by age 2; if a limb has not been used by then, the movement acquired later will never be natural. Formation of the regions that process basic vision is over by 6 months (Ratey, 2002, pp. 39–41).

Knowledge of critical periods can serve as a guide to offering certain experiences to infants and toddlers. Equally important is realizing that developmental limits, once defined as stages, are not reasons to postpone experiences until "later." How something is offered is the key to infant/toddler interest, and a far wider range of experiences are possible than formerly acknowledged.

Fall and Infants

At WBCC by mid-November the leaves were in autumn dress.

November 18. Elly brought a huge pile. The seven infants, 7 to 11 months, were attentive as she dumped them onto an expanse of burlap. They moved toward them prone, arms and legs propelling, a couple already crawling. They grabbed with two hands, crunched with one, patted, fingered a margin or vein, slid their palm along a stem, brought them close to their mouth, exploring the texture. Some quivered at the new experience. They were mesmerized when, standing on a ladder, Elly let a huge pile drift to the floor.

November 25. Elly dropped leaves on brown paper so they slid easily. Infants pushed them, swiping the leaves with their hands or feet. They examined them closely, drawn by size, shape, color, texture, sound. Today the leaves were drier, easier to crumble, crunching more loudly.

December 3. In their first explorations of pine cones, infants grabbed, turned them in their hands, probed with fingers, mouthed, dropped, banged, swiped, swung, and grasped these utterly fascinating objects, stimulating connections among eye/finger/hand/arm/shoulder movements.

An assorted palette of leaves is presented on a tray to infants, 5 to 8 months old, who explore their color, texture, and odor by grasping, holding, smelling, tearing, tasting, and in the process crushing and crumbling them.

Photos by Elly Solomon

Fall and Toddlers

The toddlers were ready for fall this year.

October 10. At the park 22- to 29-month-old toddlers walked around the trees, felt the grass with their fingers, picked up pieces of bark that they handed to the teachers, and put bark, twigs, stones, seed pods, leaves—whatever eyes noticed and hands collected—into bags teachers had ready.

November 17. Dori Weathersbee [teacher] encouraged the toddlers to use soft movements—placing precisely, swirling gently, tipping slowly—when adding leaves to the water table.

November 19. Dori watched four children gather, sort, crunch, and store leaves. She brought them together and they layered leaves between stacks of tiles to flatten them.

November 20. Today all the toddlers collected pine cones and leaves. Zaida Revilla [teacher] and Dori, thinking of beginning a fall collage, engaged them in searching for materials and discussing their choices. The children narrated, saying "hard," "new here," "listen it," "it big, big," "oooh! tickle!"

November 21. We talked about what we collected yesterday. Toddlers held pine cones, really excited, as we read the book *Red Leaf, Yellow Leaf.* Zaida and Dori decided to make many outdoor explorations before beginning a collage they had in mind.

November 24. Dori provided a clear plastic rectangular container of water: "Whenever we explore with water, the children become very excited." She encouraged them to swirl their hands slowly through the water, to immerse the pine cones gently, submerge them gradually. She demonstrated many different, precise movements.

Dalila: "Pine cone, wet. Put it in the water."
Reginold: "Pine cone, in the water," then he stopped to examine a small piece of the pine cone that had stuck to his finger.

The children liked moving pine cones in and out of water and holding them up to watch water drip. They also enjoyed cleaning up, sponging water from the table and floor.

Infants' and toddlers' attention is easily captured. Natural materials evoke nuanced movements and sensory responses that, through repeated experiences, gradually shape the brain. In children who are innately disposed, the naturalist instinct that Howard Gardner counts among humans' multiple intelligences is stimulated by these experiences.

CONCLUSION: THE POWER AND PLEASURE OF NATURE

> A society that ignores how denuding forests affects the quality of air, how manufac-
> turing poisons affects the quality of water, how destroying plants and animal species
> affects the complexity of our planetary home is not likely to lead us forward. . . . If we
> wish to have a society in which freedom coexists with responsibility, we must ensure
> that the environment in which young people grow up provides complex experiences.
> . . . Perhaps the most urgent task facing us is to create a new educational curriculum
> that will make each child aware. . .that life in the universe is interdependent. (Csik-
> szentmihalyi, 1993, pp. 269–275)

Awareness starts as wonder, which teachers can fan into passion. Infants first experience natural materials sitting on moss, grass, petals, leaves, soil, propelling
their bodies across them, noticing, grasping, handling. Toddlers run on pine needles, bark, and dirt, over hillocks, through puddles. Each material evokes movements and visual and tactile responses that differ in numerous, subtle ways. By
6 months infants have full command of the visual system. By 12 months toddlers
stoop to observe whatever is on a path. Older toddlers become quiet as they
handle chicks, hamsters, snakes, crickets, or newts. They explore the nonrecti-
linear forms of rocks and shells. They notice the alphabet of nature's lines, sizes,
textures, colors, tastes, and sounds. Sprouting seeds cause daily exclamation,
growing plants elicit close observation, and animals rouse deep emotions, the
bases for later interest in geology, biology, and botany. Entire curricula lie in a
cubic foot of soil. Toddlers eagerly share their enthusiasm about living things
with whomever will listen, developing communicative skills and stowing impressions for later years.

On a field trip Dana, age 2½, stood transfixed at the huge incubator at the Chi-
cago Museum of Science and Industry, watching chicks peck out of their shells every few minutes. Usually unresponsive, as most toddlers are when asked, "What
did you do in school today?" Dana could not contain herself: "Mommy! We saw
baby chicks. And they were in the eggs, there were hundreds of eggs, and the
incubator keeps them juuust soooo warm. Then the egg cracks. Then this little
peck, peck, peck. Then the chick comes out!" Dana repeated the same story to her
father, and to her brother, and the next day to her grandma, to the mail carrier, to
the cashier at the grocery store, to anyone she came across, with detail, precision,
and glee. That is the power of natural materials in the repertoire of a toddler's
experience.

10

Light and Shadow

Swift as a shadow, short as any dream . . . so quick bright things come to
confusion.

—William Shakespeare (1594)

From birth children confront light and shadows. Like holes, shadows exist
only because of concrete objects. They are confusing because they represent a
paradox—existence and nonexistence. In classic experiments that established
our understanding of how infants perceive objects, Spelke (1990) found that by
5 months they correctly interpret an object as something that moves as a whole,
maintains shape and size as it moves, and acts on other objects only on contact. But, in further experiments Rubenstein and Spelke (1998) found that 5- to
8-month-olds were confused by shadows' behavior.

Shadows' movements disorient the brain, causing a need to restore equilib-
rium. In this chapter I describe further aspects of how we see, discuss the nature of
light and shadow, and show ways to use light and shadow to provoke infants and
toddlers to think creatively.

HOW WE KNOW WHAT WE SEE

We know what we see because brain systems, in a fraction of a second, dissect
and reassemble complex visual scenes. Throughout our lives, the brain learns to
ascribe meaning to what the eyes see.

Marvelous Vision

Stop what you're doing and look around. As you looked up:

- Your eyes meticulously dissected the image that fell on your retina into
  approximately 126 million pieces.
- Your retina sent signals for every one of these tiny elements to a way station in
  the thalamus.
- The thalamus fired neuronal networks to and within the visual cortex.

145

- Faster than you can read this, your brain put the pieces back together into the image that fell on your retina. (Ratey, 2002, p. 99)

This complex parallel processing occurs along independent pathways in several systems. Each processes different information:

- shape,
- color,
- movement, location, and spatial organization.

The computer screen on your desk is "seen" by the visual system as a geometric shape encompassing many other shapes—the alphanumeric symbols, the icons. The blinking cursor is a separate image. Yet, you perceive everything as one. We see meaning in visual experiences because of the information exchange in the cortex where, in highly convoluted folds, visual messages combine with messages from other senses and with memory (Ratey, 2002).

In the thalamus deep within the brain are two clusters of nerve cells. Each sends waves—40 per second—throughout the brain. "The output from one allows the brain to bind together the body's ever-changing sensory inputs; the other's synchronizes the brain's internal workings" (Pollack, 1999, p. 47).

> The sweep of the forty-cycle wave through the brain is like the sweep of sunrise or sunset over the surface of the earth. As the boundary between light and dark sweeps over the turning face of the planet, a longitudinal slice of people go to bed or wake up in phase with one another. . . . What is true for people on the planet is true for the different centers of nerve cells in each of our heads. [On earth] coincidence in the instant of arrival of a global signal, not anatomical nearness, synchronizes . . . [behavior]. . . . [In the brain] synchrony between the forty-cycle-per-second clocks of the brain and a sensory organ is essential for the stability of the wiring between the senses and the brain. (p. 48)

Understanding what we see depends on what we have experienced. What must 6-month-olds, so new to the world, "see" when they look around? One of the brain's amazing capacities is that within 12 months toddlers understand what they see so well that they can name it.

Using Light as a Material

Although we cannot touch or smell it, light has texture, color, composition, and geometry that can all be manipulated. Using light teachers can:

- permanently alter an area's ambience;
- have a one-time *big* experience;
- momentarily startle the visual system;
- treat light as a material that infants and toddlers can manipulate.

Knowing which goal you are pursuing helps you clarify the intent of what you do. Changing ceiling lights has a long-term effect because it affects mood. Arousing the brain by startling it has a short-term effect because the effect diminishes once the brain becomes familiar with it.

A Constant Surround. Light is so constant and total a surround that unless a ballast flickers, a bulb burns out, or power fails, we barely think about it. Light changes a 3-year-old's middle-of-the-night walk to her parents' bedroom from a terrifying to a reassuring journey. Light influences how we perceive the aesthetic aspects of our environment and our emotional response to our surroundings.

Feelings of delight or sluggishness, fear or buoyancy, "are loosely linked to . . . [light's] quantity and quality" (Domus, 1998, p. 46). Daylight tells us what the weather is and what hour it is, as it did in the ages before thermometers and clocks. In the classroom natural light is easy to filter, screen, or texture. It can be changed with simple items like screening, sheer fabric, or colored plexiglas that children can lift, place, and shift. Daylight is thus a *living material* to handle, configure, and reconfigure, thereby changing the mood and the aesthetics of a space. Children can make the "lightscape" (Domus, 1998, p. 46) alive, spooky, or ambiguous depending on whether they use intense, cool, warm, colored, filtered, or shaded light, and on how they vary its grain (Domus, 1998). The different qualities of daylight and artificial light can be manipulated separately or combined to vary effects in the lightscape.

Altering Artificial Light. Schools generally prize uniform light and so cover the ceiling with fluorescent fixtures; their *cold white* bulbs and metal baffles are ubiquitous. Changing tubes (there are several standard tones, including *warm white*) or covering them with colored plastic sleeves (sold by lighting suppliers) changes the light quality. It can radically alter the character of the space but is a big investment of time and money, not something you can make at home and present the next morning.

Adding warm areas is easy with small bedside-type lamps that use warm white bulbs. Like any addition, many factors influence the decision: What defines the space where the lamp will be? What differences might a lamp make to activities? How will it alter the ambiance? Can it be added safely?

Altering Daylight. Window shades or translucent screens diffuse light in different ways. Blinds create linear patterns. Inexpensive sheer fabric, securely mounted, can be moved by a whisper fan to create subtle changes in the quality of light. Putting materials directly on windows is an easier way to cause effects. For example, regularly spaced holes in black paper make sunlight fall in a pattern, or theater gels create colored effects that differ on sunny and cloudy days.

October 8: Cloudy Day. Zeze, almost 3 years old, looked at the floor and gasped: "*Oh my God*! Aaaaah! The colors off the floor!" Looking at the window to be sure the colors were still there, then back down: "Aaahh! The color not on the floor.

The shadows made by colored gels on a window arrest infants' and toddlers' attention.

Photo by Jennifer Azzariti

They gone!" Knowing nothing of the relation between sunlight and shadows, he was disoriented. Renowned psychologist Reuven Feuerstein says feeling disoriented is an essential prerequisite for learning, that to learn we must notice that something is different from what we expect, and be bothered by the difference: "The origins of reflective thinking lie in perplexity, confusion, or doubt" (Dewey, 1933, cited in Lewin-Benham, 2008, p. 32).

A child's confusion provides teachers' most pregnant moments, when they can ask questions like: "Where do you think the colors *are*? Do you think they'll be back tomorrow?" Then, on the next day: "Shall we see if the colors are here today?" The teacher, like an administrative assistant to children's brains, reminds, refocuses, and provokes them to remember.

Once you begin to consider lighting effects, ideas pop up everywhere—in sculpture, theater, and movies. In art: Painters have played with light since Cro Magnon man painted bison on undulating cave walls, positioning them so that, by flickering torch light, they appeared to move (Pfeiffer, 1982). Photographers create drama by manipulating light. In the cityscape: High-rise buildings and commercially appointed interiors alter light by virtue of regular patterns on large surfaces. Open brick work, lattice fences, shower doors, Japanese screens, and row crops are all inspiring sources for lighting effects.

What Are Shadows?

Shadows lend a mysterious air to space. They are cognitively provocative and can cause memories or form questions that rattle around the brain for years.

Ambiance. Shadows make familiar spaces new, different, dark, enigmatic, secretive, or frightening. Each effect results from the relationships among:

- the source of the shadow,
- the features of the environment,
- how furniture and other objects are arranged.

> Shadows have material characteristics: they can be diaphanous and almost impercep-
> tible, which is typical of misty landscapes, or create more contrasting and volumetric
> [impressions] . . . with an almost sculptural harmony. . . . They may appear ordered or
> disordered, deforming or defining our perception of the space. (Domus, 1998, p. 51)

Where is the sun at 10 a.m. in relation to my classroom? What can I use to block its
rays so a shadow appears where there is usually light? Will infants crawling across
the carpet notice the new shadow? Will they notice their *own* shadow? How will
they react? Teachers can provoke infants to explore naturally occurring or teacher-
made shadows. They can induce toddlers to notice and create relationships between object and light source. And shadows are free, there for the using.

Cognition. Shadows are a phenomenon

> . . . on the edge of everyday experience. . . . [Children] have a vast background acquain-
> tance; but they have seldom put the lamp, the object, and its shadow in that simple pro-
> jective relation that has been there all along . . . [but] has seldom been closely observed.
> . . . [T]he times to be spent with such things, in classroom or out, must be generously
> allotted. (Hawkins, 1983, p. 76)

Hawkins calls a certain kind of knowing "apperception." It means background
experience with phenomena (light, shadow, gravity, momentum, inertia, astrono-
my, geometry, mechanics) that children meet frequently as they play. Apperception begins to develop in the infant/toddler years. In Hawkins's (1965) words,
they "mess about"—"free, unguided, exploratory" (p. 7). Unless they have plenty
of time to mess about, they will not accumulate enough experience to develop formal understanding. Appreciation of science or math concepts, of historic trends,
or of any large pattern or long time scale requires "big generalizations" (p. 8). To
think big thoughts requires "the content of experience and the logic of experimen-
tation" (p. 10), with the support of a knowledgeable teacher who sets the stage by
designing the classroom, selecting materials, orchestrating experiences, and col-
laborating in explorations.

The Role of School. Schooling must begin with messing about. To do so
classrooms must incorporate materials and teachers must orchestrate experiences
so children can continue to explore what they have met outside of school. In real-
life experiences, Hawkins (1965) says, are found "the roots of their moral, intellectual, and aesthetic development" (p. 8). In time messing about "becomes a way of
working that is no longer childish, though it remains always childlike, the kind of
self-disciplined probing and exploring that is the essence of creativity" (p. 8).

Why discuss this in a book on infants and toddlers? From birth thinking has
a cognitive dimension. Infants and toddlers are curious about everything, ready
to explore, and increasingly able to ponder. They notice nuance, perceive conflict,
wonder. These natural tendencies are gifts to teachers. When teachers set up relationships that cause disequilibrium and encourage open-ended exploration, they

enable infants and toddlers to build apperception—the kind of knowing that is grounded in extended experience and that Hawkins considers the foundation for later learning. We do not (at least not yet) program infants/toddlers, script our dialogue with them, or expect right answers. So, in the first 3 years time is open for them to explore.

DISCOVERING LIGHT AND SHADOW

Children sense right from the beginning that shadow is a "significant presence whose sense and meaning are yet to be discovered" (Spaggiari, 2000, p. 9). Here I describe a way to begin, suggest useful equipment, and then return to the World Bank Children's Center (WBCC) and to a Reggio classroom to watch infants and toddlers discover light and shadow.

Beginning

Light and shadow play requires some preparation. Certain pieces of equipment are essential props. Most important are teachers' attention to the ever-present possibilities for interactions with light and shadow, a sense of fun, and a yen for exploration.

Teachers. One way to begin exploring light and shadow is at a teachers' meeting where each in turn recounts a memory, as far back in childhood as s/he can reach, of shadows. My memory is of a car ride after July 4th fireworks, long after bedtime. I was 4 years old. Across my body light and shadow fell in an unceasing parade of vertical lines caused by headlights' beams hitting regularly spaced light poles. At first the moving images were frightening, but when I realized they would not hurt me, their constant rhythm, which became monotonous, lulled me to sleep. Equally vivid is a memory of my son, about 6 or 7 months old. Having recently mastered sitting, he was on the carpet intent on a beam of sunlight directly before him. Arm extended, he repeatedly grasped at the small patch but each time came up empty-handed. His interest was heightened when the sunlight winked (some random cloud), and waned only when the sky clouded over.

Tapping into their own childhood, relating it to colleagues, and hearing others' memories provide teachers with powerful connections to children's experiences with shadows. (Try it, you will be amazed at what you hear.) It makes it clear why shadows attract children. Once aware, teachers find themselves observing children in new ways, watching for occasions when infants and toddlers discover shapes formed by shadows—on the high chair, on the floor, in their crib, on the wall, outdoors.

Equipment. Several relatively inexpensive items make light and shadow readily available.

- A light table, described below, is first a place for infants to pull up on, crawl over, and explore, but quickly becomes a way for infants to notice how light interacts with and changes different materials.
- A wall washer enables you to play with shadows without completely darkening the room. It is a halide or low-voltage halogen incandescent lamp in a tough metal housing (insulated so you can handle it), reflective inside. It has a good spread and uniformly illuminates a wall or screen at some distance. Wall washers provide sharp, clear shadows. Their mobility enables you to easily change the distance between light source and screen. Check the Web or lighting suppliers. Be sure the lamp you select has enough lumens to be bright at a distance.
- An overhead projector combines a magnifying lens, projecting lens, light source, and *bed*. Placing objects or images on the bed provides endless opportunities to create and manipulate light and shadow.
- A screen is a staple in Reggio classrooms. Screens can be made from a cloth, with cords attached, that rolls into a wooden housing and mounts to the ceiling. Cords can be found where drapery materials are sold; salespeople usually know about size, weight, and assembly. Buy sharp white fabric with no pattern, smooth and heavier than sheets; sew a wooden bat into the bottom edge so it hangs straight. A white wall will do but only for shadow play. With a screen children can be either actors from behind or audience in front.

Experiences

The same ingenuity we saw with man-made materials (see Chapters 4 and 8) is evident in the WBCC's explorations of light and shadow.

Using Light with Infants. Infants from 5 months to 10 months use a light table and overhead projector for the first time.

On December 19 we brought the light table to the infant room. The table is small—20 inches by 23 inches and only 6 inches high. At first we thought it would work best in a darkened area away from other activity. We had just such a *found* space. We put it there, no materials, just the table itself. The infants who could crawl were on it immediately. Since all the children wanted access, the space was too restrictive. On December 31, our second trial, we removed the table from the enclosure. To find a place that would allow access from three sides, we rearranged the entire room. This time we provided flat white, translucent sheets. Infants who could pull up moved them all over the table.

The transparent plastic fruit containers [see Chapter 3] were ideal on the light table. We filled many with different arrays of material that were either shiny, reflective, translucent, or transparent. With the edges taped, infants are unable to open the containers, but even before 6 months can grasp, slide, lift, shake, and wave them. The combination of light, color, sound, and the powerful feeling of lifting something so large made them irresistible. We made many of them and moved the light table again to give infants access from four sides. (Elly Solomon, studio teacher)

January 16: Light Table and Holes. We used pencils to punch holes in sturdy black paper, using a pegboard, exactly the size of the table top, as a guide. The pegboard kept the paper from ripping. The effect was a dark grid with small bright circles, their luminescence intensified by the black paper.

Sometimes there is nothing on the light table and the infants bring a material; other times we brainstorm what to use. We have laminated lengths of string and yarn and strips of construction paper. We have used fabric with a loose weave, CDs, paper towels, and "gems" in compartmented plastic containers. The infants become very excited when they see us carrying materials to the light table; they fall silent, watch us intently, and follow. We do not have time to set up the materials because they dive into them so quickly. (Elly Solomon, studio teacher)

March 27: Overhead Projector, First Use.

We decided this was the time to use the overhead because we saw an infant notice then try to grab the shadow her hand made on the tray [high chair]. We let the infants explore the projector itself. They investigated the entire machine, including the vents. Then we turned it on and put a bangle bracelet that a teacher happened to be wearing onto the bed. The infants looked back and forth from object to wall. Some tried to catch what they saw on the wall. (Elly Solomon, studio teacher)

March 30: Light Table and Moonsand. Elly put moonsand (see Appendix A) in a large, clear plastic container with a transparent bottom. Moonsand falls apart easily when touched but clumps readily when squeezed. The light became hazy when infants swept their hand over the sand and disappeared where they dropped squeezed sand.

April 2: Overhead Projector and Magnetic Tiles. The head of the projector grabbed the infants' attention. They looked at it, turning it every which way, realizing that the mirror disappears when you close the housing. Four classrooms share one projector, so each uses it once a week. Today, the infants' second use, we noticed that they made a connection between the overhead and the image on the wall.

Ivan, 12 months, sat at the projector moving around magnetic tiles [standard school supply]. Once he realized that they stuck together, he combined tiles before putting them on the bed. Sergio, 13 months, watched Ivan's hands intently. The minute a shape appeared on the wall, he went to touch it. Ada and Roland, both 8 months old, looked long and hard at the images.

April 16: Light Table and Magnetic Tiles. The magnetic tiles glow when illuminated. The children "clicked" the magnets against one another and "swooshed" them across the table. They were attracted simultaneously by the sound and color, and were riveted watching what their classmates did.

Using Light with Toddlers. The 15- to 21-month-old toddlers had different experiences exploring light and shadow.

November 26: Light Table. Six children clustered around the large light table in the hall using transparent colored magnetic squares, triangles, and other shapes [standard preschool materials]. Some built a tower, while others placed shapes side by side, their constructions more complex than the infants' but their attraction to this pleasing material magnified by combining the shapes with light.

January 9: Light Table and Clay. We placed small slabs [3" x 3"] of clay on the light table to cover it. Dmitri, 22 months, turned on the light. Dalila, 23 months, Juan, 17 months, and Dmitri laughed, becoming excited.

When we gave them wooden sticks [flat and too thin to scratch the surface], they started to poke the clay. Adam, 20 months, seeing the light come through, exclaimed, "Light!" then began poking until the slabs fell apart. One narrated:

Dalila: "Poking the clay, dots."
Dmitri: "Clay, patting clay."
Reginold, 22 months, cutting into the clay with the wooden stick:
    "Reginold cut, Reginold cut."

These toddlers from 17 to 23 months scratch, scrape, pick, and peel clay off the bed of the overhead projector and realize that when they remove the clay they can see the light.

Photos by Jessica Gagliardi

Toddlers explore the effects of circles and lines projected on the wall by feeling the images as their teacher moves different objects.

Photos by Jessica Gagliardi

Mahaly, 21 months, held a slab in his hand, a good grip for poking.
  He broke the slab in half, then began to tear small pieces that he
  explored with his fingers.
Juan watched, focused and very quiet.

January 12: Overhead Projector and a Variety of Objects.

I selected a variety of objects that I tested to make sure their effects were interesting when projected. Some were circular—linked circles [lightweight wooden chain from a room separator], a pegboard; others were linear—a pillow tassel, a length of yarn and a strand from the tassel, a linear grid [metal dish drainer]. I kept these objects in a basket beside the projector.

Reginold and Dmitri had used the projector months earlier; for the others it was the first experience. The instant he saw the shadow on the wall, Reginold tried to match the object, quickly figuring out what was making the shadows, intentionally placing objects so they would project, and checking back and forth from object to wall. He was the only child who seemed certain that putting an object on the projector made a shadow on the wall. Dalila broke into a long, continuous smile, exclaiming: "Circles!" All the children pointed at the shapes, recognizing many. We encouraged Edwina, 17 months, and Juan to look and touch the wall. Juan supported himself by holding onto the wall, absorbed in the images moving in front of him.

This toddler makes the connection between placing an object on the bed and seeing its image on the wall. Each time he puts a new object on the bed, he turns to see the effect.

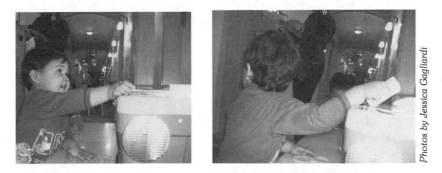

Photos by Jessica Gagliardi

On their own initiative Adam and Dmitri chose bubble wrap bags and scrubbed the images. Adam, at a stage when he liked cleaning tables with paper towels, continued throughout the entire experience, about 20 minutes. Dmitri laughed when he saw the shadow the pegboard made. I dropped the tassel on the bed and moved it a bit. It was very dramatic. Dalila and Reginold, the oldest toddlers, cried, "Spider!" and Dalila started singing "Itsy Bitsy Spider." As I moved the tassel, Mahaly was captivated watching the shadows. Dmitri pointed at them: "Moving! Moving!"

When I realized how the movement riveted the children's attention, I began to move objects that would have a big effect. The wooden chain appeared to move across the room! Infants who had not been taking much notice were immediately alerted and started paying attention. Reginold and Dalila began to take objects from the container to move by themselves. When I put the pegboard on the bed, the wall went dark. It was really dramatic; all you could see were little holes. "Oooh!" Dalila exclaimed, "What's that?" Dmitri, pointing at them: "Wow!" We encouraged the children to touch the "holes" on the wall. Dalila began pointing and counting. I moved different objects across the bed. Edwina watched closely, pointing as images moved across the wall. The children were fascinated, excited, intent. (Jessica Gagliardi, studio teacher)

One toddler decides to scrub the image with a bag made from bubble wrap, an object that also changes under the projector's intense light.

Photo by Jessica Gagliardi

January 21: Light and Paint.

The children painted on diaper-changing paper that, on the light table, became translucent. Dori [teacher] used bright pink paint. The color was even brighter with light glowing from beneath.

I decided to repeat the experience [projector and objects] with other classes of 2-year-olds. The reactions were different in each class. One had its own projector so had had a *lot* of experience, but their materials were ordinary. Yet, even when I brought more interesting materials, they had their backs to the wall, uninterested in the shadows, so different from the toddlers' first experience. The 2-year-olds were interested in choosing new materials to put on the bed of the projector. They spent a lot of time selecting and arranging, one day assorted materials, another day string, still another day an assortment of new materials, each time for almost 20 minutes. Only when I moved the chain did a shadow catch their attention. They laughed, trying to catch it. (Jessica Gagliardi, studio teacher)

February 27: Bags of Material and Overhead Projector. Jessica sealed materials into sheet protectors—seed beads, sequins, glitter, small square colored shapes, shiny shapes. Edwina moved close to the bed and moved sequins around with her finger. She and Reginold looked at the huge shadows the materials created. Reginold was more interested in watching his own shadow as he moved.

Dori to Reginold: "What's on the wall?"
Reginold: "Dmitri's hand."

The teachers wondered what the children's reactions would be to using markers with projected images. They fastened large paper to the wall, projected an image of connected plastic rings (the kind that are used in packaging soda bottles and cans) and gave the children black markers. The 2-year-olds made an immediate connection and took the tops off their markers. They made scribbles—near, but not necessarily related to, the circles.

The toddler has placed a pouch with glisteny objects on the bed of the overhead projector and finds that they glisten even more when he moves them.

Photo by Jessica Gagliardi

At first the toddlers scribbled, but as they become aware of the many spots of light cast by the pegboard (right), they change their scribbling to circle making.

Photos by Jessica Gagliardi

Jessica continues:

We decided to try the pegboard that the children always found exciting. A few days later, we again fastened large paper to the wall and projected the pegboard. Alonso and Carissa were extremely excited. We offered them black paint and brushes with long handles. At first they scribbled, but seemingly all of a sudden, Alonso reached as high as he could and filled a circle just within his reach with a circular mark! Carissa followed suit and a rash of circle drawing ensued. When they had filled the marks within reach, Carissa repositioned the pegboard on the projector bed so they could reach to fill more circles! Her action showed us that she understood that there was a relationship between where the image lay on the projector bed and where it fell on the wall. We were excited that both children made a transformation—outlining the bright circles with paint in a form recognizable as a circle.

These early experiences with light and shadow are rich. They grab children's attention, keep it focused, and challenge eye, hand, and fingers to coordinate. The challenge to teachers is where to go next. Experiences in Reggio schools offer some ideas.

Shadow Play in Reggio

At Il Girotonda 21 toddlers gathered in front of the floor-length screen. From behind the teacher began projecting slides, exotic images of sea life. "Ooohs" and "aahs" erupted, the toddlers keenly attentive to the slowly changing images for more than 30 minutes.

The teacher brought a few toddlers behind the screen, encouraging them to move with the images, until half the group participated while the other half watched. Gradually more joined the performance—toddlers silhouetted among sea life. Then the teacher introduced props on handles—cut-out fish, starfish, plants. She encouraged the toddlers to engage their props with the images and one another's props. Now spectators saw a dance of children and sea creatures. Another 30 minutes passed.

Changing the tenor, the teacher showed slides of an empty grey ocean and a gigantic shark. She introduced a new prop, a shark's head that one child immediately put on. She encouraged the "shark" to chase the "small fish." The toddlers shrieked as shark-child chased fish-children. As the chase subsided, the teacher collected the props. Over an hour had passed. She turned on the lights and independently the toddlers became involved in other activities (Lewin-Benham, 2006).

CONCLUSION: ENTICING THE INFANT/TODDLER BRAIN

Shadow play in Reggio is an art form. When inventive experiences with light and shadow are used repeatedly, they offer children ways to fulfill maturational imperatives—aligning different parts of the body to function seamlessly, experiencing cognitive conflict that stimulates theory-making, transforming shadows by painting, drawing, moving, and tricking them. Experiences trigger the brain functions that from 0 to 3 lay the groundwork for increasingly complex learning. Work by 5- and 6-year-olds in Reggio schools is remarkable—original, creative, complex, and competent—the hallmarks of significant work. The skill with which it is executed shows the influence of their experiences from 0 to 3.

I hope the stories in this book have shown the critical role of materials. I hope the stories have explained what it means for teachers to be intentional, to listen to children's interests, to be responsive to them, and to feel joy as they do. I hope they show possibilities for teachers' own inventiveness. I hope they showcase the role of aesthetic experience. Above all I hope the stories inspire a wave of meaning-full activity based on a belief in the competence of infants and toddlers. When this happens, we will have powerful schools. They will yield evidence that we have indeed harnessed the power of the brain to find relationships, and of the hand to express those relationships in a great variety of creative ways. Each child's forming relationships and building his own skill set is, after all, the most powerful evidence of human's creative capacity.

Essential cognitive skills children learn from using materials are:

- restraint of impulsivity,
- reduction of egocentric behavior,
- sustained attention,
- categorizing skills,
- planning,
- use of summative behavior,

- analytic ability,
- precision,
- use of time and space.

For years I saved a large collection of "stuff"—package closures, raffia, bottle tops, broken jewelry. Sheppy, at 3 and 4 years old, had sorted it, making his own connections as he classified and stored the items away. For years he used the collection as a resource for many self-initiated projects. In 3rd grade and having just turned 9, he asked: "SeeSaw (his name for me), I have a science project and need to go to the attic; there are things there I cannot find anywhere."

When the brain contains a large vocabulary of materials, it is like having cabinets full of treasure. With this treasure a child can imagine, build relationships, realize ideas for projects, make constructions and contraptions, and in a word *think*. That is the outcome of using materials with infants and toddlers.

Appendix A: List of Materials

Aluminum
Bark, fallen from trees
Baskets, like strawberries come in
Beads
Bits of tinsel
Blank paper (see Paper)
Bolts
Bottles, transparent, little or no writing (see Glass jars):
  • From flavorings, like vanilla
  • From perfume, lotion, shampoo
Bottles, hotel-sized. If you don't stay in hotels, ask a traveling friend to save empties.
Boxes, small, hard, like jewelry boxes
Brads
Brass
Bric-a-brac
Brushes, assorted—pastry brush, vegetable scrubber, basting brush, nail brush, toothbrush
Bubble wands, that make varied bubbles, tiny to huge
Bubble wrap
Buttons, snaps, eyehooks
Cards, greeting and postal (used) with interesting images
Cardboard tubes, assorted lengths and circumferences
Cardboard, all sizes and thicknesses, including corrugated

Casters
CDs
Cellophane candy wrappers, ends untwisted, smoothed
Cereal containers, cylindrical
Charms
Clamps
Clear boxes, all types
Clipboard
Clips—mini-paper clips, fat binder clips, every other kind
Coffee cans with lids
Computer or typewriter keyboard letters (no sharp parts)
Contact paper
Containers—yogurt, cottage cheese, transparent plastic egg and fruit cartons
Copper
Corks
Costume jewelry
Cupcake papers/muffin papers
Dowels, short, long, thick, thin, plexi, wooden, metal
Dried beans, grains, rice
Dried flowers
Elastic
Empty foil-lined bags
Envelopes, all sizes
Eraser—MAGIC RUB® works best
Fabric

Fasteners—paper clips, brads, grommets

Firm fruits and vegetables, plum-size and larger, thoroughly washed, peeled

Fishing line (monofilament)

Fishing tackle (hooks removed)

Floral wire

Flowers—fresh, pressed, dried, silk

Foil wrappers from candy or other foodstuffs, surfaces smoothed

Foils, silver and colored

Game pieces

Gears, from clocks, appliances, machines

Gift wrap, used and leftovers

Glass jars, all shapes and sizes, little or no writing or labels

Glues
  - Elmer's all purpose (not school glue)
  - Glue sticks
  - Wood glue

Hardware—rubber and metal washers, nuts and bolts, eyehooks, swivels, odd pieces

Jar tops

Jute

Keys

Labels—blank, dots, florescent

Lace

Lace paper doilies

Leather laces, strips, and pieces

Lengths of waxed, freezer, parchment, or other paper

Markers (see Appendix B)

Mesh bags like produce comes in

Mirror toy with hexagonal frame. Source: Apple School Supply (http://appleschoolsupply.com/lookatmemirror.aspx)

Moonsand, a material that clumps together like sand when moist but is not messy. Source: Discount School Supply (http://www.discount schoolsupply.com/Product/ProductDetail.aspx?product=25801)

Nails

Needles and needle threader

New sponges (no hard backing, none soft enough to pull off pieces)

Nuts, hardware and from trees

Paper cups

Paper of all types in different thickness, opacity, reflectivity, color, size, and finish—shiny, transparent, blank, lined, squared, patterned, embossed:
  - Card stock (see Appendix B)
  - Construction
  - Fadeless art paper
  - Gift wrap
  - Heavy brown
  - Newsprint
  - Packaging
  - Tissue
  - Tracing
  - Typing
  - Wallpaper (stores give old sample books)
  - Watercolor paper
  - White, varied weights, finishes, sizes

Paper bags

Paper plates

Pebbles

Pencils, #1 and #2 black lead

Pencils, varied colors. Be sure they are soft enough to leave a rich trace of color (see Appendix B)

Petri dishes

Plastic containers, clear and colored

Plastic fasteners, flat, varied colors (as used in packaging bread)

Plastic flower pots

Plastic straws

Plexi pieces, mirrored, clear, colored, all shapes, sizes, thicknesses

Postage stamps, canceled

Pots and pans

Push pins, clear and colored

Raffia, natural and colored

Ribbon—endless varieties, recycled from gifts

Rubber bands, widely assorted sizes and colors

Rubber stamps

Rulers, 6", 12", and 18"

Scissors—Fiskar's® best scissors for children; tips are rounded, blades really cut.

Scraps of soft wood

Screw eyes

Screws

Seam binding

Seed packets for collage

Seeds and pods

Sequins, bugle beads

Shells

Silk flowers

Silver foil

Skwish, classic baby toy. Source: http://www.manhattantoy.com/ product/296210/200970/_/Skwish_ Classic

Slides, blank and with images

Small-sized tools that really work, no plastic

Soil, repotting quality

Spoons, a variety of sizes, shapes, and substances

Spray bottles, clear glass or plastic

Springs

Stamps, postage (canceled) or promotional

Stickers, not commercial but free with junk mail. Cut off the name/address, keep the picture.

Stones

String

Styrofoam trays from meat or fish packages

Tape, assorted widths and colors; cellophane, cloth, masking, metal

Tassels

Telephone wire

Thimbles

Thread

Thumbtacks

Trims

Tubing, clear or opaque, rubber and plastic (clean)

Twigs

Twist ties, the longer the better

Vases

Veneer

Wallpaper (see Paper)

Washers

Wire, thin and thick, very flexible; brass, silver, copper, colored, plastic:
- Aluminum screen
- Chicken wire
- Copper screen
- Plastic mesh
- Wire mesh

Wood curls

Wood details (finials, trims, moldings)

Wood scraps, sanded on all surfaces and edges

Wrappers, shiny metallic

Yarn

Zippers

Appendix B: Art Supplies

This list includes items not likely to be found at home or that have to be purchased from an art supply store.

Acrylic paint, introductory tube set (about $10–$14)

Beads/buttons/collage materials

Brushes, different sizes and styles: flat, round, watercolor, Chinese watercolor

Card stock: various weights, colors, and sizes

Chalk: thick and thin, varied colors

Charcoal

Chinese watercolor

Clay-shaping tools, wooden or plastic (sold as a set)

Clay: low-fire, white or terra cotta

Clay wire cutter

Colored papers (see also Paper in Appendix A)

Colored pencils, 24–48 (Prismacolor, Lyra, Faber-Castell, or Prang are good brands; Derwent is incredible but extremely expensive)

Crayons, 48–100

Decorative papers (see also Paper in Appendix A)

Dura-Lar, clear acetate, 5 millimeters thick; widely available on the Web

Gel medium (puts a shiny coat on paint or clay or adds a protective layer to acrylic paint; or use it to extend acrylics)

Markers: thick and thin point, varied colors

Mat board scraps (check a local frame shop)

Oil pastels

Painting paper (50 lb. weight works well), a source for good paper is http://www.dickblick.com/products/blick-white-sulphite-drawing-paper/

Palettes, may be called paint trays (use for mixing acrylics, water colors, or inks)

Paper (see Appendix A)

Pastels

Pencils in a range of hardness: 2H, 2B, 4B (H is hard, B is soft); Faber Castell or Derwent are good brands.

Pens: black fine-line, ballpoint, UniBall

Rolling pin, wooden; small (for child), large (for adult)

Tempera paint: red, yellow, blue, black, and white

Watercolors: cake and liquid

Water-based inks; Windsor-Newton makes beautiful inks.

Appendix C: Tools

It is useful to have these in child and adult sizes. It is critical for a child's tool to really work. Try before buying.

Clamps
Cutting mat (sold by that name in art
    supply stores)
Exacto knife (for adult use only)
Funnel
Glue gun
Hammer
Hole punch
Mortar and pestle
Needle threader
Paper cutter, old-fashioned with ruled
    "bed" and arm. Be sure children

cannot reach.
Pencil sharpener
Scissors
Screwdriver
Tape measure
Wire cutters
Wood working tools and equipment
Wrench
Yardstick

Glossary

Aesthetic: Visually appealing, sensing what is beautiful.

Apperception: Initial experiences with how light, water, balance, or any physical entity behaves; these experiences are essential for eventually understanding a phenomenon.

Atelier, Studio: A room, like an artist or craftsperson uses, for work or production. It contains equipment, tools, and a good supply of materials.

Atelierista, Studio Teacher: An artist or craftsperson, skilled in the use of materials and tools, who as a teacher brings the artist's point of view to a school.

Attention: A system, part of the brain's executive functions, that alerts the brain, selects, and maintains focus on stimuli. It is an essential part of every act.

Brain stem: The structure above the spinal cord at the base of the brain that regulates functions like breathing, digestion, and heart rate.

Cortex, cerebral cortex: The deeply folded outer covering of the brain. It is divided into four areas, called lobes.

Critical periods: Times when specific brain developments take place before the brain prunes connections; missing a critical period makes it more difficult, or impossible, to acquire the function.

Disequilibrium: A feeling of being disoriented or off balance.

Endorphins: A neurotransmittor (chemical released by the brain's pituitary gland) that reduces pain and produces feelings of well-being.

Explicit memory: "The storage of information about people, places, and things that requires conscious attention for recall . . . [and] can be described in words" (Kandel, 2006, p. 437). It is converted to long-term memories in the hippocampus for storage in other regions of the brain.

Flow: Deep involvement in an activity that blocks out interruptions and produces peak performance and joy.

Framing: Presenting an experience so that the brain is alerted that something is about to happen that requires attention.

Frontal cortex, frontal lobe: The area responsible for the brain's executive functions, speech, planning, and movement.

Gustatory: The sense of taste.

Haptic: The sense of touch combined with movement.

Implicit (or procedural) memory: "The storage of information that does not require conscious attention for recall" (Kandel, 2006, p. 440); memory of routines or habits such as dressing, cooking, or riding a bike. They are stored in the cerebellum, striatum, or amygdala.

Kiln (pron. kill): An oven used to process, or "fire," clay at very high heat. A kiln is extremely heavy and usually kept outdoors because of the high temperatures generated.

Lightscape: The atmosphere created by manipulating daylight and/or artificial light sources.

Limbic system: A set of systems deep in the brain commonly associated with emotion; thought to regulate the four "F's"—including fearing, fleeing, and feeding.

Maturational imperative: A basic human drive to breathe, move, crawl, eat, speak, and relate to other humans, for example.

Mentalese: A word that denotes the way a brain communicates with itself. It in no way resembles language but is a "hypothetical 'language of thought'" (Pinker, 1994, p. 509).

Mirror neurons: The recently identified brain cells that are activated as someone watches another's actions. They are considered responsible for imitative behavior.

Mnemonist: A person with exceptionally good memory.

Modality: Any way in which humans receive or express information; for examples, verbal, graphical, motoric, and all forms of signs and symbols.

Motor cortex: The area of the cortex that receives motor sensations and is involved in relaying nerve impulses to muscles.

Neural network, also called circuit: "A group of several neurons that are interconnected to and communicate with one another" (Kandel, 2006, p. 442).

Neuronal connection: The firing of a synapse or release of a chemical that makes it possible for brain cells to communicate.

Neuron: "The fundamental unit of any nervous system . . .[with] the unique ability to communicate rapidly with one another over great distances and with great precision" (Kandel, 2006, p. 443).

Neuroplasticity: The tendency and capacity of the brain to rewire itself as the result of repeated experience.

Olfactory: The sense of smell.

Photon: The basic unit of light; it activates the photoreceptors in the visual cortex.

Prefrontal cortex: The most forward part of the cortex, responsible for higher-level thinking such as attention, planning, and decision making.

Proprioception, proprioceptive: The body's ability to sense its location and position in space.

Reciprocity: The responsive behavior that can be initiated by either mother or infant and that is their form of communication.

Reggio Emilia: A small city in northern Italy renowned for having the world's best infant/toddler centers and preschools.

Reticular activating system: The part of the brain stem that receives sensations from the skin and certain joints and senses and as a result keeps us conscious and aware.

Retinal cell: A specialized cell in the light-sensitive lining of the eye that forwards visual information for processing.

Schemata: Any "unified, overarching mental representation that helps us work with a topic or subject" (Perkins, 1992, p. 80).

Self-regulation: Part of the brain's attention system, an executive function that enables children to control attention as well as all other behaviors, including concentration.

Slip: A mixture of clay and water, used to attach pieces of clay to one another.

Soliloquy: A technique in which an adult speaks while engaged in an activity so a child can hear the approach and solution.

Synapse: The site between two neurons where either chemical or electrical impulses pass from one neuron to the other.

Somatosensory cortex: The portion of the cerebral cortex and the brain system that processes sensations from the body surface of "touch, vibration, pressure, pain, and the sense of limb position" (Kandel, 2006, p. 449).

Stimulus, stimuli: Any object, sensation, or experience that arouses a response from the brain.

Synesthesia: When one sense produces the response of another; for example, hearing sound but seeing color.

Thalamus: Relays most of the information from the sensory and motor systems in the brain to other parts of the brain.

Visual cortex, occipital cortex: The visual processing center of the brain.

References

Alvaro, F. (2008). Training emotion and self-regulation: Interview with Michael Posner. *Sharp Brains*. Retrieved June 9, 2009, from http://www.sharpbrains.com/blog/2008/10/18/training-attention-and-emotional-self-regulation-interview-with-michael-posner/

Beebe, B., Alson, D., Jaffe, J., Feldstein, S., & Crown, C. (1988, May). Vocal congruence in mother-infant play. *Journal of Psycholinguistic Research, 17*(3), 245–259.

Berk, L. (1994). Brain development in young children: The early years ARE learning years. In D. Ramsburg (Ed.), *Resources* (pp. 1–3). Urbana-Champaign, IL: Clearinghouse on Early Education and Parenting. Retrieved June 2, 2009, from http://ceep.crc.uiuc.edu/pubs/ivpaguide/appendix/ramsburg-braindev.pdf

Berk, L., & Winsler, A. (1995). *Scaffolding children's learning: Vygotsky and early childhood education*. Washington, DC: National Association for the Education of Young Children.

Bruner, J. (1996). *The culture of education*. Cambridge, MA: Harvard University Press.

Campbell, D. (2000). *The Mozart effect for children: Awakening your child's mind, health, and creativity with music*. New York: HarperCollins.

Carey, S. G., & Gelman, R. G. (1991). *The epigenesis of mind: Essays on biology and cognition*. Hillsdale, NJ: Erlbaum.

Chugani, H. (2004). Fine-tuning the baby brain. New York: The Dana Foundation. Retrieved January 8, 2009, from http://www.dana.org/printerfriendly.aspx?id=1228

Chukovsky, K. (1963). *From two to five*. Berkeley: University of California Press.

Collinson, S. (2002). Philosopher of the month: Kenneth Craik. *The Philosophers' Magazine*. Retrieved February 23, 2008, from http://www.philosophers.co.uk/cafe/phil_sep2002.htm

Conrad, J. (1897). *The nigger of the narcissus*. Retrieved June 1, 2009, from http://www.classicauthors.net/conrad/Narcissus/Narcissus1.html

Csikszentmihalyi, M. (1990). *Flow: The psychology of optimal experience*. New York: HarperCollins.

Csikszentmihalyi, M. (1993). *The evolving self: A psychology for the third millennium*. New York: HarperCollins.

Damasio, A. (1994). *Descartes' error: Emotion, reason, and the human brain*. New York: Quill.

Dobbs, D. (2006, October). Big answers from little people: Psychologist Liz Spelke plumbs the depths of infant cognition. *Scientific American Mind*. Retrieved June 20, 2009, from http://daviddobbs.net/page2/page3/page3.html

Dolci, M. (2000). Shadows: From myths to tricks. In *Everything has a shadow except ants*. Reggio Emilia, Italy: Reggio Children.

Domus Academy Research Center. (1998). *Children, spaces, relations: Metaproject for an environment for young children* (G. Ceppi & M. Zini, Eds.). Reggio Emilia, Italy: Reggio Children.

Edwards, C., Gandini, L., & Forman, G. (1998). *The hundred languages of children* (2nd ed.). Norwood, NJ: Ablex.

Eisner, E. (2002). *The arts and the creation of mind*. New Haven, CT: Yale University Press.

Emerson, R. W. (1912). The rhodora. *Yale book of American verse* (T. R. Lounsbury, Ed.). New Haven, CT: Yale University Press. Retrieved June 3, 2009, from http://www.bartleby.com/102/38.html

Families and Work Institute. (2009). *Mind in the making: National campaign—an overview*. Washington, DC: Author.

Feuerstein, F., Falik, L., & Feuerstein, R. (in press). *Mediated soliloquy: Theory, concept and a monograph series*. Jerusalem: International Center for the Enhancement of Learning Potential.

Feuerstein, R., Feuerstein, R. S., Falik, L., & Rand, Y. (2006). *The Feuerstein instrumental enrichment program: Part I and Part II*. Jerusalem: International Center for the Enhancement of Learning Potential.

Fontanili, M. (2007). *Play +: Soft furniture for children*. Reggio Emilia, Italy: Reggio Children.

Galinsky, E. (2010). *Minds in the making: The seven essential life skills every child needs*. New York: Harper Studio.

Gallese, V., Fadiga, L., Fogassi, L., & Rizzolatti, G. (1996). Action recognition in the premotor cortex. *Brain, 119*, 593–609. Retrieved February 19, 2008, from http://www.unipr.it/arpa/mirror/english/staff/rizzolat.htm

Gardner, H. (1980). *Artful scribbles: The significance of children's drawings*. New York: Basic Books.

Gardner, H. (1991). *The unschooled mind: How children think and how schools should teach*. New York: Basic Books.

Gazzaniga, M. (2008). Arts and cognition: Findings hint at relationships. In Dana Consortium, *Learning, arts, and the brain: The Dana Consortium report on arts and cognition* (M. Gazzaniga, C. Asbury, & B. Rich, Eds., pp. v–viii). New York: Dana Press.

Gelman, R., & Au, T. (1996). Perceptual and cognitive development. In E. Carterette & M. Friedman (Eds.), *Handbook of perception and cognition XIII* (2nd ed., pp. 3–43). San Diego, CA: Academic Press.

Gelman, R., & Shatz, M. (1977). Appropriate speech adjustments: The operation of conversational constraints on talk to two-year-olds. In M. Lewis & L. Rosenblum (Eds.), *Interaction, conversation and the development of language* (pp. 27–63). New York: Wiley.

Hawkins, D. (1965). *Curriculum and instruction in arts and education* (E. Engel & J. Hausman, Eds.). St. Louis, MO: CEMREL (Central Midwestern Regional Educational Lab).

Hawkins, D. (1974). *The informed vision: Essays on learning and human nature.* New York: Schocken.

Hawkins, D. (1981). Enlargement of the aesthetic. In S. Madeja (Ed.), *Curriculum and instruction in arts and aesthetic education* (pp. xii, 22–32). St. Louis, MO: McREL.

Hawkins, D. (1983, Spring). Nature closely observed: Scientific literacy. *Daedalus, Journal of the American Academy of Arts and Sciences, 112*(2), 65–89.

Hawkins, F. P. (1986). *The logic of action.* Boulder: Colorado Associated University Press.

Huttenlocher, J., Haight, W., Bryk, A., Seltzer, M., & Lyons, T. (1991). Early vocabulary growth: Relation to language input and gender. *Developmental Psychology, 27,* 236–248.

Kandel, E. (2001). *Eric R. Kandel: Autobiography.* Retrieved May 28, 2009, from http://nobelprize.org/nobel_prizes/medicine/laureates/2000/kandel-autobio.html

Kandel, E. (2006). *In search of memory: The emergence of a new science of mind.* New York: Norton.

Klein, L. G., & Knitzer, J. (2007). Promoting effective early learning: What every policymaker and educator should know. *Effective preschool curricula and teaching strategies.* Columbia University, National Center for Children in Poverty. Retrieved July 11, 2007, from http://nccp.org/publications/pub_695.html

Lewin-Benham, A. (2006). *Possible schools: The Reggio Approach to urban education.* New York: Teachers College Press.

Lewin-Benham, A. (2008). *Powerful children: Understanding how to teach and learn using the Reggio Approach.* New York: Teachers College Press.

Malaguzzi, L. (1991). *Little ones of the silent pictures.* Reggio Emilia, Italy: Reggio Children.

Malaguzzi, L. (1995). *Shoe and meter: Children and measurement, first approaches to the discovery, function, and use of measurement.* Reggio Emilia, Italy: Reggio Children.

Merzenich, M. (2004). *Michael Merzenich on rewiring the brain.* Retrieved May 28, 2009, from http://www.ted.com/index.php/talks/michael_merzenich_on_the_elastic_brain.html

Merzenich, M., Nelson, R., Kaas, J., Stryker, M., Jenkins, W., Zook, J., Cynader, M., & Schoppmann, A. (1987, April 8). Variability in hand surface representation in areas 3b and 1 in adult owl and squirrel monkeys. *Journal of Comparative Neurology, 258*(2), 281–296. Retrieved June 15, 2009, from http://www.ncbi.nlm.nih.gov/pubmed/3584541

Mix, K., Huttenlocher, J., & Levine, S. (2002). *Quantitative development in infancy and early childhood.* New York: Oxford University Press.

Montessori, M. (1967). *The absorbent mind* (C. A. Claremont, Trans.). New York: Henry Holt.

Neville, H., Andersson, A., Bagdade, O., Bell, T., Currin, J., Fanning, J., Klein, S., Lauinger, B., Pakulak, E., Paulsen, D., Sabourin, L., Stevens, C., Sundborg, S., & Yamada, Y. (2008). Effects of music training on brain and cognitive development in under-privileged 3- to 5-year-old children: Preliminary results. In Dana Consortium, *Learning, arts, and the brain: The Dana Consortium report on arts and cognition* (M. Gazzaniga, C. Asbury, & B. Rich, Eds., pp. 105–116). New York: Dana Press.

Ornstein, R., & Thompson, R. (1984). *The amazing brain.* Boston: Houghton Mifflin.

Perkins, D. (1992). *Smart schools.* New York: Free Press.

Pfeiffer, J. (1982). *The creative explosion: An inquiry into the origins of art and religion.* New York: Harper & Row.

Pinker, S. (1994). *The language instinct: How the mind creates language.* New York: HarperCollins.

Pinker, S. (1997). *How the mind works.* New York: Norton.

Pollack, R. (1999). *The missing moment: How the unconscious shapes modern science.* New York: Houghton Mifflin.

Posner, M. (2004). *Cognitive neuroscience of attention.* New York: Guilford Press.

Posner, M., Rothbart, M., Sheese, B., & Kieras, J. (2008). How arts training influences cognition. In Dana Consortium, *Learning, arts and the brain: The Dana Consortium report on arts and cognition* (M. Gazzaniga, C. Asbury, & B. Rich, Eds., pp. 1–10). New York: Dana Press.

Ratey, J. (2002). *A user's guide to the brain: Perception, attention, and the four theaters of the brain.* New York: Vintage Books.

Reggio Children. (2004). *Children, arts, artists: The expressive languages of children, the artistic language of Alberto Burri.* Reggio Emilia, Italy: Author.

Rinaldi, C. (2006). *In dialogue with Reggio Emilia: Listening, researching and learning.* London: Routledge.

Rubenstein, J., & Spelke, E. (1998). Infant sensitivity to shadow motions. *Cognitive Development, 13*(4), 387–419.

Sacajawea Interpretive Center. (2009). *Text panels.* Olympia: Washington State Parks and Recreation Commission.

Sacks, O. (1996). *The island of the colorblind.* New York: Knopf.

Sacks, O. (2007). *Musicophilia: Tales of music and the brain.* New York: Vintage Books.

Shakespeare, W. (1980). A midsummer-night's dream (Act 1, Scene 1, Lines 144–149). In D. Bevington (Ed.), *The complete works of Shakespeare* (3rd ed.). Glenview, IL: Scott, Foresman. (Original work published 1594)

Shonkoff, J., & Phillips, D. (Eds.). (2000). *From neurons to neighborhoods: The science of early childhood development.* Washington, DC: National Academy Press.

Spaggiari, S. (2000). To be amazed by children. In *Everything has a shadow except ants.* Reggio Emilia, Italy: Reggio Children.

Spanish phonemes. (n.d.). Retrieved March 27, 2008, from http://help.lumenvox.com/robo/projects/speechengine/programmers_guide/SRGS/phonemes/spanish_phonemes.htm

Spelke, E. (1985). Preferential looking methods as tools for the study of cognition in infancy. In G. Gottlieb & N. Krasnegor (Eds.), *Measurement of audition and vision in the first year of postnatal life* (pp. 323–363). Norwood, NJ: Ablex.

Spelke, E. (1990). Principles of object perception. *Cognitive Science, 14*(1), 29–56. Retrieved January 6, 2009, from http://www.telegraph.co.uk/scienceandtechnology/science/sciencenews/3341166/Harvard's-baby-brain-research-lab.html

Spelke, E. (1998). Nativism, empiricism, and the origins of knowledge. *Infant Behavior and Development, 21,* 181–200.

Spelke, E., & Kinzler, K. (2007). Core knowledge. *Developmental Science, 10*(1), 89–96. Retrieved June 6, 2009, from http://www.wjh.harvard.edu/~lds/pdfs/SpelkeKinzler07.pdf

Starkey, P., Spelke, E. S., & Gelman, R. (1990). Numerical abstraction by human infants. *Cognition, 36,* 97–127.

Wilson, F. R. (1998). *The hand: How its use shapes the brain, language, and human culture.* New York: Pantheon Books.

Index

About the Author

Ann Lewin-Benham has been mother, teacher, teacher educator, grandmother, and author. In the 1960s, with a group of parents, she expanded a Montessori preschool into an elementary school. As the children approached junior high school age, she spearheaded the founding of Parkmont Junior High School, located today in Washington, D.C. In the mid-1970s she became frustrated with the seemingly impossible task of changing the paradigm of school practice for all but a small fraction of students. So, she left formal education. For the next 20 years she worked in informal education, founding and running the Capital Children's Museum located in a riot-torn area in Washington, D.C. By the mid-1980s she realized that museums could not replace schools. In the museum's rambling buildings she began again, founding the Model Early Learning Center (MELC) for 3- to 6-year-olds, and the Options School, a dropout prevention junior high for 7th graders who ranged from 14 to 18 years old. Her first two books, *Possible Schools* and *Powerful Children*, tell the story of the MELC. It is the only school outside Reggio Emilia, Italy, ever accredited by the renowned early childhood schools of that city. For more information about Ann's lectures, teacher workshops, and writing, visit her website, AnnLewin-Benham.com